Soccer For Thinkers

Malcolm Allison

ACKNOWLEDGEMENTS

Cult Figure Publishing would like to thank Gerry Harrison (who worked with Malcolm in the initial writing of this book) and Malcolm's family for their help in republishing this book. Also, Tony Book and Colin Bell MBE, for both kindly providing a foreword to Soccer For Thinkers.

For more information on Cult Figure Publishing and other titles they have published, as well as future projects, please visit the website at: www.cultfigurepublishing.com

Cover design by Digital Print Shop.

CONTENTS

Acknowledgements
Preface by Rob Finch
Preface by Gerry Harrison
Foreword by Colin Bell MBE
Foreword by Tony Book

SOCCER FOR THINKERS

PART 1: THE TEAM

PART 2: THE PLAYER

Part 3: THE TEAM PLAYER

PREFACE TO SOCCER FOR THINKERS

BY

ROB FINCH

The reader is asked to bear in mind that this book was first published in 1967. The text remains unaltered and as Malcolm wrote it back then. They are asked to take that context into consideration, as it explains why the players referenced and some of the concepts used are applicable to that era. It is also worth considering, as it will highlight how revolutionary and forward thinking a football coach Malcolm Allison was. Many of the ideas explored in the book were at the time highly innovative and subsequently became the norm - a testament to Malcolm's abilities as a football thinker.

It could be argued that Malcolm's colourful persona and unsuccessful spells as a manager often overshadow his standing in the game. However the book demonstrates that beneath the famed fedora and underneath a cloud of Cuban cigar smoke, what a brilliant coach he was. It also further highlights the differences between a manager and a coach. Some of football's most successful managers have done little to no coaching - they bring different skills to the dressing room. Malcolm was very much a football coach and whilst history tells us that Malcolm may not have been one of football's best managers, he was certainly one of the greatest coaches the game has seen..

Malcolm began his coaching career whilst still a player at West Ham United. After joining the club from Charlton Athletic, he soon gained a reputation for ideas and innovations and was encouraged by then manager Ted Fenton, to employ his theories on the youth and junior teams. Malcolm found a willing student in the shape of the young Bobby Moore - to whom he became a mentor.

His theories eventually played their part in the evolvement of West Ham being known as the 'Academy of football'. It saw the club nurture some of the greatest talent in British football history, producing Bobby Moore, Martin Peters and Geoff Hurst, to name but three players, who enjoyed long and illustrious careers at club and international level.

Malcolm's most successful era, was as a coach in conjunction with Joe Mercer at Manchester City. Where - in a hugely successful five year period, the club won the Second Division Championship (the equivalent of The Championship), the First Division League Championship, (the equivalent of The Premier League), The FA Cup, Football League Cup and UEFA Cup Winners Cup.

Whilst at City, his theories and coaching ability enhanced the careers of players like Tony Book who he plucked from non-league football and Colin Bell - who later enjoyed international recognition. Little wonder that Mercer called Malcolm: 'The greatest coach in the world'.

The book is designed to be a guide to help improve the performance of players of all ages and abilities. As a guide to help coaches get the best from players and for the uninitiated to better understand the reasons how players who perform at an elite professional level do so. Those readers who are looking for lurid accounts of Malcolm's colourful off-field persona may be disappointed. However those looking to get inside the mind of one of the beautiful games most innovative and forward thinking coaches have come to the right place.

PREFACE TO SOCCER FOR THINKERS

BY

GERRY HARRISON

Soccer for Thinkers may look a little old fashioned today, but many of Malcolm Allison's ideas and coaching techniques were breaking new ground in the 1960s. Much of his thinking has stood the test of time and despite the huge changes in the game, on and off the field, a lot of it is just as relevant today as it was then.

It was a great education for me to listen to Malcolm talk football, watch him at work with Manchester City and then knock that into some sort of written shape. I'd got to know him when he was at West Ham and starting out on a coaching career. When I moved to Manchester as a news reporter on the Daily Express, we met up again and he suggested the coaching book. There were no shortage of takers and we placed the idea easily. After all, Malcolm was the 60s version of Jose Mourinho in a fedora, City were the most exciting side in the country and Joe Mercer had established a club which, as he put it 'lived and played with a smile.' He had taken the City job only on condition that Malcolm was hired as his coach. 'He's the best in the world' he said. 'My job is to protect him from himself'.

The hardest aspect of compiling this book was keeping pace with Malcolm's movements. His limitless energy meant a full day of coaching and training with senior players and juniors, was followed by scouting missions. Around all that, he fitted in a social life which would have left the Rat Pack on their knees. In the end, I found it easier to catch Malcolm as he came home in the early morning and stick with him until training started.

Near deadline day, I had gone looking for him in one of Manchester's many night clubs. I failed to find him and wasted my last five pounds on the blackjack table. As I left the club, a taxi pulled up and Malcolm stepped out. 'Come on in,' he insisted. ' Let's get that sweeper system sorted out.' I pleaded poverty and just wanted to fix a definite time for the next day.

He wouldn't hear of it, stuffing some notes into my top pocket, he then made a stylish entry into the club. It seemed a hundred people wanted to greet him. We talked for a while, then some young actresses from Coronation Street spotted him and called him over and he was gone. 'Tomorrow - eight - thirty, the training ground' he shouted. And he was on time - with a few notes he had made the night before. I subsequently discovered he had borrowed the money he gave me from the taxi-driver.

Malcolm wasn't serious about too much - except his football ideas. He insisted this coaching book was straight forward football - no scurrilous or racy anecdotes to make it attractive for newspaper serialization. And he had plenty of those. He wasn't inspired to write the book by money either, just a love of football. On initial release, Soccer For Thinkers was very well received in the game at many different levels. I hope a new audience finds it similarly useful. Malcolm deserves it, for as a football coach he was one of the very best.

FOREWORD TO SOCCER FOR THINKERS

BY

COLIN BELL MBE

There is no doubt that my career as a football player benefitted from having worked with Malcolm. In fact I would say that anyone who worked with Malcolm would end up a better player as his coaching ideas were that good. The man lived and breathed football and was always thinking of new ideas and new approaches to the game. He was way ahead of his time too.

When I played at Bury, the training was fairly standard but under Malcolm it was something different every day. We often changed the environment where we trained and did our training in different places. Malcolm always kept things fresh and was always looking at different ways to help us improve as players. He was always encouraging us and had a knack for getting the best out of people.

He took inspiration from different areas too - not just football. He was always looking for different ways to help us improve. For example, I remember on one occasion he had been studying the training methods of the successful sprinter Valeri Borzov - who won two gold medals at the Olympic Games and he used a few things that he found there in our training sessions.

From the first time I met Malcolm, he was always thinking about football. Even after he retired from the game he never stopped. I remember going to see him many years after he had retired from the game. He was in hospital and not in the best of health - suddenly he perked up and started talking about a new system he was working on - I couldn't believe it, but I shouldn't have been surprised.

People's perceptions of Malcolm are often based on the more flamboyant side of his personality but you would not find a more dedicated man, nor would you find anyone with a greater gift for coaching football players. It was a shame that he did not get the chance to coach the England national team as I know he would have done a brilliant job. To me it was England's loss, as Malcolm was a fantastic character and a brilliant football coach.

FOREWORD TO SOCCER FOR THINKERS

BY

TONY BOOK

I first met Malcolm when I was playing at Bath City. He had just finished playing at West Ham United and came to the club as the manager. It was instantly clear that he was on another level and light years ahead of what we had been doing previously.

He couldn't believe that we only trained a couple of times during the week and he soon upped that to five times a week. He believed that practice and proper training was the key to our development as players and he was right. He definitely improved me as a player.

It was Malcolm, who gave me a chance in professional football and at thirty years of age, I made my football league debut for him when he got the manager's job at Plymouth Argyle. Two years later he took me with him to Manchester City and our success there was down to Malcolm's coaching methods and Joe Mercer's management style.

I would go so far as to say that Malcolm was way ahead of his time and that he looked at the game differently to how other people did. Training with Malcolm was always lively and he was always coming up with little drills and exercises to make it interesting.

I was very much his guinea-pig and he used to have me doing all sorts of things. When other clubs were doing very basic training, Malcolm had me wired up to a running machine at the local university for fitness analysis. He was also big on things like getting blood tests and looking at the medical side of it too. All things that are very much the norm now but unheard of back then.

Despite that, Malcolm believed that football was a simple game that should be played the 'right' way and at Manchester City I think we did just that. When he came to the club, Malcolm had a tough act to compete with, as our rivals at Manchester United had the great Sir Matt Busby in charge and of course he had some wonderful players at his disposal. Malcolm had to make an impact and with some great coaching methods - many of which are in this book and with his flamboyant personality, he did just that.

CHAPTER ONE

The First Aim

The final judgement of almost everything in football, results, standard of skill, attraction, strength and even behaviour, is through the team. Individual players stick in the memory. But Eusebio, Moore or Suarez could not make a school 2nd XI without ten others to support them.

It appals me that soccer is taught in so many places with the game's priorities in the reverse order. Most coaches, when they take charge of a group of players, immediately begin by teaching skills. Skills are vital, but they are only important in the context of the team's game. If a boy cannot spell a simple word he is letting himself down. If he cannot trap a simple ball he is letting his team down. The team comes first and trapping is part of that team.

When I take over a group of players to coach them, regardless of age or physique, my first object is quite simple—to make them appreciate that it is a team game.

The formula for this at any level is through different sorts of conditioned games—that is, games in which the coach imposes a restriction of some kind on the players.

Restrictions obviously affect the good player most because his skills will be limited. But the lesser skilled player will learn very quickly, if he has it in him, how he can play a more useful role in the team.

Get a game of *One Touch* going—full pitch, 22 players, a proper game. The individuality of each player is immediately sacrificed. The severity of the restriction evens things out. Strength, speed and ball skill mean very little. Even at a professional level in an ill-disciplined side the first minutes might be chaos . . . until they see their only escape.

11

It is usually as much as three-quarters of an hour with boys aged thirteen or fourteen before the game begins to flow. Until then few will enjoy it. It will look awful. There will be a great deal of inaccuracy. But keep it going. Don't give up too early. A coach must never start something and give up half-way.

The player appreciates there are others around him he must use. He must look and see where they are before he gives a pass, before he receives the ball. His one chance of getting into the game is by finding a clear position. The game becomes open only when players appreciate the value of this basic positional play. The individual sees some of his limitations as a member of a team. It is no good being a breath-taking individual dribbler if your own defence cannot find you with a pass. A centre-forward with an explosive shot is useless if he is always hidden behind the centre-half. The only way to play this game is as a team.

The coach appreciates which of the players sees situations quickest and best. He sees who the workers are. He sees sometimes that the player with all the skill in the world at his command has no idea of how to become a useful part of a unit.

The object is to produce in the fastest possible time the basis of sound team play—understanding and cohesion. Without the complication of involved explanations the footballer will be introduced to the craftsman's technique of reading the game, and that instinctive knowledge of what is going on around him.

Two Touch. This introduces elements of skill and control and use of the body in feinting, and changing direction. It also teaches the value of being able to take your eye off the ball— and when keeping your eye on the ball is not only a disadvantage but a mistake.

Watch any high-class match. There will be a tremendous amount of two touch play naturally in the game—instant control and unselfish positional play by the players without the ball.

At other levels this Two Touch game brings home to players even more their own lack of skill, and that their only real strength is through helping each other. To begin with, they might take three touches to control and pass. Do not let them get away with it. They, and their team, must be penalised.

Ten-yard Balls. To make young boys keep their play open, it may be necessary to impose the restriction of not making passes of less than 10 yards in one and two touch games. This encourages them to use the whole of the pitch and at the same time improves their kicking power.

All Left Foot. The majority of young players are one-footed. Play the same conditioned games, alternating the feet. Even more players, particularly as they get older, are one-eyed—under pressure certain parts of the field are blanked out to them, mainly because they have developed the habit of relying on one foot. This condition helps to break that down. Because passes with the weaker foot must be simpler to be accurate, it promotes once again intelligent positional play to make things easier.

Calling. Calling is an important part of football and should be taught as a separate skill. In one touch games or two touch games occasionally ban all calling. Silence increases the necessity of each player learning how he can help out most and how to foresee the flow of the game.

Goalkeeper. He is not a footballer. He is a handball player, and must be coached as an individual. In these conditioned games he is there to complete the team, nothing more. In these artificial situations the value of the goalkeeper to his team in difficulty or in attack should be more obvious.

Habits form away from the coach: in practice, in the dinner hour kick-about, in unsupervised games. When the coach leaves, he will be deceiving himself if he does not realise that the players will fall back into their old mistakes.

Once the players have grasped the idea of the Team Game and the primary importance of their positions in relation to the other ten, they must be taught good habits.

The next step is take off the conditions. Now INSIST they play the ball quickly, quickly, quickly in an ordinary game.

It is very important not to condition the game after the basic team idea is instilled. Playing it quickly will produce the same results in natural circumstances.

This is something they must be coached and coached to do whenever it is possible. It is a habit they must get into. Watch a good First Division team play a weaker side. The good side play the ball about quickly, appearing sometimes to make unnecessary passes. This is a habit with them, whether the opposition were fifteen-year-olds or a Fourth Division reserve side. If they begin to play it slowly their level will often sink to that of the inferior opposition.

13

The great Hungarian team of the 1950s often played full-scale practice matches against ordinary works sides. There are a number of reasons why they did this. But they were always forced through habit to play it quickly, quickly, whatever the works side was doing.

When the Football League team, virtually England's World Cup side, played the Irish League at Plymouth four months after the Final against West Germany, the Irish were overwhelmed 12–0. Newspapers always make much of the fact that the Irish are part-timers. Of course, that extra speed, strength and skill mean the Football League should always have the better players. However, it wasn't that which shattered the Irish. The players said afterwards it was the speed of the play. Not the speed of the players, the speed of the ball. When the goalkeeper, Albert Finlay, returned to Belfast he admitted, almost seriously: "You know, the first time I saw the ball was in the papers the next morning."

Why is quick play so important? It changes the situation all the time. When the ball stops, the defender's task is suddenly easier. He can weigh up the situation, pick up his man in relation to that situation, organise cover and even anticipate the next move.

But each time the ball moves from player to player the defensive picture is changed. Great individuals like George Best, Charlie Cooke or Bobby Charlton can change that picture half a dozen times in a 20-yard run—by a body movement, a feint, a hint of a pass, by changing the angle of the run, by stopping and starting. Defenders are forced to move in anticipation of where the ball is going next. It is also exceptional play and the rest of us must more often rely on quick play for the same effect.

CHAPTER TWO

Games With Possession

It is already obvious that the essence of the team game is seeing situations quickly, with each player working out how he can help the others—and then doing it.

Now break the training down into small games. This is to emphasise particular team situations in any game, first of all when your team has possession of the ball.

The object: to teach correct running, to teach what is a safe angle, what is a safe ball and when to play it. Football is all angles, with an occasional curve thrown in. Bobby Moore wanted to be a draughtsman if he had not made the grade as a professional footballer. There is really quite a similarity in the two crafts.

First, a word about running.

Running off the ball does not mean sprinting down the pitch leaving the player with the ball in isolation. It means being in the game without the ball, but prepared to receive it at any second— by running backwards, towards the man with the ball, sideways, forwards, back-pedalling towards your own goal, anywhere, not always in a straight line . . . anywhere to free yourself . . . putting yourself in a position to link up with the player who has the ball, in such a way that the two of you are taking on one defender—or as it is known technically—making it a two against one situation.

Two against One: a man with the ball and another running alongside must get past the defender. There are many things to consider. A bad defender will make for the man with the ball. A better one will try to commit himself to neither one nor the other, keeping between them and the goal, trying to close the angles up as the attackers get nearer goal.

The attackers will find interpassing is not always the best way through. More often it is safer for the man with the ball to use the one running alongside as a dummy, feinting to pass, but keeping it.

Don't forget, a bad square pass which is intercepted cuts both players out of the game. In a match it could be more.

The attacker's first instinct will be to veer his run away from the defender. He should be taught to do exactly the opposite. Run directly at him. Force him to commit himself. Good positional play, a dribble or a pass will put him out of the game.

Do it all at speed. Make it live.

Four against Two: this is played within a limited area like the centre circle, which makes it harder and makes passes tighter. Don't give less skilled players more room. Make them work for what this game demands—accuracy, sharpness, control. There are always positions to be found. There should always be two alternatives if the players are working for each other. The correct one to play is the safest. For this is a game for possession, not goals. Make the most of the technique of changing the direction of the game and of running.

Four against two is usually re-creation of mid-field situations. But it will improve the team's play in tight situations anywhere.

Turning: even at professional level turning with the ball is a highly specialised skill which demands continuous practice. Jimmy Logie of Arsenal turned better with the ball under pressure than anyone I have ever seen. Many of the great inside-forwards have this art, but not many others. We shall deal more with this later. Make it a point to play Four against Two simply and safely. With a number of players in a confined space, make the most of the technique of playing the ball the way you are facing.

This game is the foundation on which many of the best teams in the world build. Chelsea and West Ham continually work at this. So do Borrussia Dortmund, Hamburg and many of the German teams. It is a favourite in Russia. Dukla of Prague base their game on it. In the World Cup the Argentinians played it brilliantly, producing extra men in difficult situations and getting out of trouble that way. It has always been a major training practice in the Argentine.

The Numbers Game: in this game each player is numbered

from one to whatever number is playing in each side, say five a side, six a side or even seven a side. In an ordinary competitive game the ball must be played in numerical sequence. No. 1 must play it to No. 2, No. 2 to No. 3, No. 3 to No. 4 and so on. If No. 3 of the opposition intercepts in the course of the game he must play it to No. 4.

This evens the running load and makes every player run off the ball. The hard working player has less to do. It will winkle out the lazy one, those who like to hide for a spell or fade away for a breather when it suits them.

Put a lazy player in a Three against Three game—which is really a pressure practice. The other two will quickly appreciate his weakness. The coach will not need to do any goading. The grumbling from the other two players will be enough.

Play this game in any open space with makeshift goals. Seven against Seven needs a half a pitch; Three against Three something like twenty yards by thirty yards.

Time and Practice: a game is in bursts. Training should be in bursts. One of the biggest failures of English training is that if an hour is laid down on the schedule, then the coach will work the players for an hour. This is a mistake.

Footballers, particularly young ones, cannot maintain sharpness and concentration for an hour. Work in bursts—three minutes, four, five, six—then stop. Rest for two minutes. Ball juggling, anything. Then off again for five minutes. Then stop. Players can be pushed and stretched this way. Alertness and sharpness can be injected into their game.

Always work above match speed, if possible, particularly if you do not have much time for training. So that when they play a full-scale game well-trained players will be under less pressure and will be able to concentrate for ninety minutes. The only effective way of doing this is through short, sharp small games.

CHAPTER THREE

Games For Getting Possession

If your team could keep possession of the ball for ninety minutes it does not take a mathematical genius to realise there is a good chance of winning . . . although the opposition will have to have a touch or two at kick-offs. It does not work out that way, of course.

Too many players, not always just the younger ones, put themselves in a limited category—forward, an attacker; full-back, defender; centre-forward, goal scorer.

The object of these practices is to teach each player that he has two responsibilities, as an attacker and as a defender, whatever his position.

The foundation of football is really ten playing against ten with a couple of handball players thrown in. Basically it is a man for man game. It is the same whether you are playing any one of a hundred systems. Eventually it is reduced to—who is marking whom.

There's a story told about Wilf McGuinness, Manchester United's strong wing-half who had great defensive qualities.

United were playing away and leading 1–0. At half time Matt Busby detailed Wilf to keep in closer contact with an inside-forward who was looking very dangerous near goal. Five minutes from time, after some feverish activity in United's goal mouth, a driven cross riccocheted off a defender's knee straight to the feet of the inside-forward, who equalised.

In the dressing room, Matt Busby's first words, in mock anger, were to McGuinness. "Where were you, Wilf?" he asked. The wing-half took him seriously. "It wasn't my fault, boss. I was nowhere near him."

When we come to deal with tactics without possession later,

18

there is room for argument about what should be done in certain situations.

In the *Man-for-Man Marking* game (five, six, seven a side, even numbers, some sort of goal) there should be no doubt in anyone's mind. Each player has two jobs. As an attacker he must get free. As a defender he must prevent the other man getting free.

Often slow players are frightened of getting near a quicker player. Or an older player backs away from an opponent. Their fear is being beaten on the turn. They think they are giving themselves time. They feel safer—but this is making their job more difficult. Keeping a distance makes the opponent's positional play good, and he is the one who is given more time.

The man-for-man marking game disciplines the amount of running each player can do. If he runs wild in attack he will be missing when his side loses possession.

As soon as the game breaks down, the players without possession must pick up a man—and get goal-side of him. Within 30 or 40 yards of the ball the marking must be very tight. This is the area where it counts—the area where the ball is. Mark tightly in the area of the ball.

It is a hard game. The coach needs to keep a sharp eye on it. Inter-Milan play it a great deal. One of the best examples of how the principle involved helped a player and a team was when I was playing with West Ham.

As a wing-half Andy Malcolm was matched against some of the best inside forwards of the day, playing at their peak—Johnny Haynes, always finding space; Jimmy Greaves, already scoring from fractional opportunities; Ivor Allchurch, fast and creative.

Andy's natural reaction was to play them in the normal way, relying on his ability and reading of the game to be in the right place at the right time. He had to be forced into the role of really close marking, without neglecting his other duties too much.

He found that if he arrived very quickly on top of the player when the ball was anywhere in that 30, 40 yard area—the ball not necessarily coming his way—he could put any of the outstanding individuals out of the game. He always played particularly well against Haynes.

After the first success he was willing to play tight in that dan-

19

ger area whatever part of the field that was. But when we had possession he was still doing his job as an attacker.

The Numbers Game: this game, exactly as it was explained earlier, has a great value in making clear each player's marking responsibilities.

During this practice the initiative of the players on both sides is tested. Those of the side with the ball can run where they want. They have no labelled positions like right half or outside left. This encourages a certain freedom of expression to conquer the difficulty of the numbers passing sequence.

But when the game breaks down the same players cannot disappear from the game irresponsibly. Nor can they be expected to mark their opposite numbers rigidly.

Their initiative is taxed again, but as defenders this time. If one player had made a 30-yard run for a clear position and the other side gets possession, then someone else must fill in for him. Everyone must automatically get goal-side of a man. The player out of position must push himself back into the game and at least pick up the nearest player, regardless of his number.

The ball must inevitably come his way again unless it breaks down before then. The closer he marks, the better his chances of regaining it. This is anything but as simple as it sounds.

CHAPTER FOUR

Stamina and Speed

With a few minutes to go at Wembley in the World Cup Final, the ball ran towards the touch-line after Stiles had tackled Haller. "As I saw it run free I thought: 'Oh no! I can't get that one. I'm finished'," said Alan Ball. "I had already died twice and been looking for a chance to have a breather for ten minutes. That Schnellinger was already shooting after it. Well, I'd been beating him all afternoon so there was no reason why I couldn't do it again. Here we go again, I thought. This time I am really finished."

How fast he raced to the ball I could not judge. Certainly it was faster than anyone else at that particular instance. Incidentally, Sabo, one of the linkmen in the Russian team, was convinced that Ball finished the freshest man on the field, despite his inner torture.

That isolated incident illustrates more than that football is a running game which calls for bursts of speed. It goes much deeper than that. Speed is essential. But the ability to produce speed often is more essential. The basis of speed is stamina and strength. The key to the ability of being able to produce speed often is stamina and determination. It is valueless being the fastest player in the world if, after sixty minutes of a match, you haven't the strength to use it or cannot force yourself to make the effort.

Before we approach the question of orthodox speed training, we must first deal with stamina running—and the mental barriers which must be broken down.

As a player I loathed laps. The old, standard training picture paints footballers staggering out of the dressing rooms with the trainer standing in the middle of the pitch lighting a cigarette as

21

he bawls "Six laps!" This order produces a burst of groans from the players and a fit of coughing from the trainer. Off they lumber in twos and threes until the keener ones work their way to the front. "Come back here, you silly whatsits" the older players call from the back. For they know that at the end of the sixth lap the cry from the centre-circle will be: "Ten laps!"

Much as I would like to discount laps entirely, it is difficult to do so. Undeniably the running builds some sort of stamina. Enough laps are exhausting physically. Mentally, they are killers in very small doses. Laps strengthen the legs, condition the lungs and dull the brain, for there is no pressure on the players, mentally or physically.

Footballers have always feared running over long distances because it is so hard. "We are not runners," they will say, and then go out and average three or four miles each in a game.

If a player ran twenty miles a day he would be fit—but not fit for football and certainly not fit to take on the sort of situation that Alan Ball found himself in, which is, after all, a common one.

The stamina of British players of all ages is reputedly of a high standard. During the World Cup I visited most of the sixteen training camps. Much of the hard work had been completed before the squads arrived in this country, but nevertheless I was not impressed by the overall level of fitness. France, Chile, Brazil, Bulgaria, even Italy looked particularly poor; Argentina, Russia, Germany, Portugal, Korea, Hungary and England looked well-trained and strong.

Even if the standard here is quite high, and it should be in our climate, it does not compare favourably with the standards athletes set themselves.

Football's own "Hungarian Revolution" in 1953, after England's 6–3 defeat, sparked off a wave of near-hysteria in training methods. Overnight, running was out. Training became all ball skills and theory. The Hungarians themselves, of course, were great runners and in that particular international covered distances in ninety minutes which seemed unnatural for footballers of that era. Their recent World Cup players were once again fine runners. Seven of their first choice side were capable of doing the 100 metres in less than 11.7 seconds on grass.

A balance has returned to today's training methods. In many

clubs laps are back in favour. But not with me. If a player makes a 30-yard dash for a pass but it breaks down, makes a similar dash but it breaks down again, goes a third time but again it breaks down, he probably won't go the fourth time. I want to train him in such a way that he will have the determination to go again, the strength to be able to do it and the speed to beat his opponent. And I tackle this in the same way as an athlete trying to improve his sprint at the end of a race—physically and mentally.

First, a player's running must be increased. This is the easiest way of becoming almost overnight a better player. He does not necessarily have to use it all in a game, but he needs to be able to produce it when required. Old players fade out of the game because they cannot run far enough or fast enough. When Di Stefano was seventeen the Argentine coach Rigomino, the ex-Milan A.C. player, said he was the fastest thing on two legs he had ever seen. And whenever he played he continually popped up in every part of the field with seemingly inexhaustible energy. Now he no longer runs enough for the top level he is finished—but his skills and experience remain almost matchless. Without the ability to run he is nothing.

Europe's leading middle-distance runners recognise that one of the best methods of training for stamina is through Fartlek and Paarlauf running. Fartlek has changed considerably since it was first conceived by the ex-Swedish coach Gösta Holmer a quarter of a century ago. With the advice of one of Britain's finest middle-distance runners, Derek Ibbotson, and athletics coach Joe Lancaster, I have brought these methods into our training.

Fartlek is fast running, about three-quarter pace at the slowest and sprinting at the fastest, interspersed with slow running or jogging, all on a soft surface, preferably in countryside or parkland where there are hills.

Paarlauf incorporates the same idea—fast running with jogging between the runs, but performed on a track, in competition.

This form of training, I know, increases the heart muscle and has improved the running and stamina of the professionals, aged between fifteen and thirty-five, at Manchester City in only a few sessions. Who is to say whether this is the only way of training a football team? Athletes who have spent decades evolving the best system use these methods with success. Leeds, Stoke and West Ham use much the same sort of idea. Liverpool, Chelsea and Sheffield Wednesday, who are always in the best possible condition physically, probably are guided by other methods. I am quite sure, however, that identical principles will be involved—that running must be mentally and physically demanding.

Let me describe the make-up of a morning's stamina training for twenty-six players of all sizes and ages devised by Derek Ibbotson and coach Joe Lancaster specifically for footballers' purposes.

A mile gentle warm-up in track suits or protective clothing is followed by loosening exercises; then, in groups, over 100 yards, half a dozen times at three-quarter speed, gradually accelerating at the end; hopping, 50 yards on one leg, the rest on the other, over two 100-yard stretches.

The players are already breathing heavily. This is where the work begins and every player is ready to discard his heavier clothing whatever the weather.

A two-mile Fartlek: through fields, woods and parkland, The players are split up into two or three groups, Derek Ibbotson leading the first group, who are the club's best runners. Thirty yards behind, the second group, usually the younger players, has a good runner at the front and another at the rear to chase up stragglers. Every time the leader opens up or slows or sprints the group must follow. The maximum distance Ibbotson accelerates for is 150 yards; the shortest, a sprint, varies between 20 yards and 50 yards. There must never be any walking. No orders are given. The eyes must tell the legs what to do.

If the groups are too big the players straggle out and only the front runners change their pace. The back ones merely keep pace. The jogging distance between bursts is varied according to the strength and fitness of players. The ordinary runner will feel the strain very quickly and it is increased by having to watch what someone else does and copy it. The poor runner, in fact, sprints farther than anyone else.

Paarlauf: In the time it takes to organise the players into twos, a good runner with a bad runner or two average runners together, they will have had enough recovery time for the next effort—this time on the 440-yard track.

The distance, if run in repetition, which produces fitness in the quickest time is 220 yards, a theory substantiated by athlete's scientific research. This next exercise is a Paarlauf of six laps split between the pairs so that each player completes six 220 yards. Half the runners begin on the starting line and race 220 yards to touch their partner across the other side.

Before the other man has completed the lap and reached the original starting line the first runner must jog across the middle to be ready to run again when he arrives. In the same way the second man must jog back to his original starting-point.

The difficulties, mental and physical, are jogging across the track with one eye on the other runner . . . there is no time for walking . . . and starting the 220-yard race. This needs a lot of determination and quite often a helping hand, vocally, from the coach.

At the fourth session Manchester City players completed this distance in times varying between 6 minutes 43 seconds and 6 minutes 52 seconds, showing an improvement each session.

After a short recovery period the two main groups were led off on another Fartlek of a similar distance, but this time performed quicker. This, of course, relies entirely on the ability of the front runner.

The second time we did this training, after the players had completed that Fartlek, they thought quite reasonably that training was over. I thought they were capable of more, and Derek Ibbotson wanted to show them the importance of breaking down the mental barrier. So we went straight into a three-lap Paarlauf. The players were not keen and our trainer, John Hart, a very experienced player and a disciple of fitness, said he thought they were at their limit and would not be able to do the exercise properly. Everyone was amazed when after a three-lap Paarlauf the times recorded were faster, comparatively, than in the first Paarlauf.

I cite this example, not to advertise the superiority of our players or methods. Footballers are much the same everywhere. It is important because it demonstrated to those players above all the depth of stamina and speed even the slowest man can reach if that mental barrier which says "No, I can't do it" can be broken.

In a match there is no stop-watch, no company of sufferers,

no Derek Ibbotson to lead, no coach to bully from the side lines
—just determination and stamina. This method of stamina
training, which we do once a week in the winter, is, I am sure,
the most interesting and efficient way.

Most clubs do stamina training at the beginning of each season and a certain amount should be introduced into early
schedules. I prefer to do the bulk of it in the winter. When the
weather, the light and the grass are at their best it seems a
mistake to neglect any opportunity of getting outside and
concentrating on ball skills, competitive games and tactics which
involve sitting around. In winter, when the grounds are heavy,
stamina is much more in demand. Players need to keep on the
move and running is one aspect of training which can be performed in the half light or even the dark.

Sprints and the quest for speed should be a feature of training all the year round for anyone with any ambition, however
modest, of being a player.

Every forward needs to be quick; full-backs should be equal
at least to the speed of wingers. Players calling genuine pace
into their game less often must have exceptional skills to prevent their lack of speed being a serious liability to their side.

Football calls for a variety of speeds—genuine pace over
longer distances of the kind which wins races, short bursts, even
a couple of strides made more rapidly than an opponent.

Once again the secret of success has two factors, one physical,
the other mental. The physical aspect is obviously the ability to
get off the mark and put one leg in front of the other faster than
the next man. Quite often coaches and trainers concentrate
exclusively on this element of speed running. I think this is a
mistake. Mental alertness, determination and the ability to read
the game will frequently win him the ball and give him the
appearance of being a speedy player when technically he should
be classed as an unexceptional runner. When two players run together the one who says "Go" will win a sprint. Speed training
should always take into consideration the importance of increasing a player's sharpness equally as much as his speed, to
give him the same sort of advantage in a match that saying
"Go" gave him in training. It is not easy.

There is a success story demonstrating this question of determination and speed, of mind over matter, which has a ring of

imaginative fiction about it (except that it is true), and has left behind a basis of hard fact which has come to be an excellent practice for forwards in the penalty area.

As a boy of seventeen Stanley Mortensen was one of the slowest players on Blackpool's books. "You are so dreadfully slow," he was told more than once, "it is only luck which keeps you here." He was playing left half in the "A" side at the time and when he was moved to centre-forward his lack of speed was even more apparent. He determined to do something about it. Normal training seemed to do nothing for him. "I had to become a speedy player," he said, "otherwise I knew I wouldn't make the grade. And being as slow as I was, I knew it meant a tremendous amount of work."

There was something else which drove him on. "I dreamed about playing for England, despite what everyone said."

So he devised his own simple sprint programme off the field. On the field he would chase the balls that everyone else had given up as hopeless and try to make them his own.

His training required getting someone else to help him—anyone who was capable of kicking a ball. Both stood on the edge of the penalty area. When his co-opted help kicked the ball forward Mortensen had to sprint to it and control it before it crossed the goal line. That simple practice involved the vital ingredients of speed, power and match play . . . a start, a stop with the ball as the important object, and physical limitations, the lines, to make it harder.

Time and again he repeated the movement. More often than not he could not reach the ball before it crossed the line. But however it was kicked, he went for it. His judgement of a ball's pace improved with his sprinting.

This practice of his own he linked with the other players' normal sprints. Another favourite of his was running along the Golden Mile on the Blackpool front at the height of the season, dodging in and out of the pedestrians. "You need very quick reactions to keep yourself out of trouble doing that," he said.

But the hardest and best practice was the penalty area—goalline sprint with the target a ball. Within a year he had made an impact as a fast centre-forward. "To a lot of people the improvement was dramatic," he says. "But to me it was slow and very hard work."

27

From then on Stan Mortensen was always a player renowned for his short dash and feared for his ability of making something from hopeless balls that nobody else wanted. "There were thousands I couldn't have got even if I had been a greyhound. But I kept trying for them."

In 1948, England were playing Italy in Turin. It was a match of great international prestige value. Mortensen's dream of playing for England had come true long before and his was a name that sprang to mind whenever his club mate Stan Matthews was mentioned. In Turin they were once again on the same side.

"Stan Matthews gave me a pass which left me clear 40 yards out. Off I went, but I could feel a defender catching me up. I slowed down to let him close on me. Then I was going to sprint away and leave him when he thought he had me. Just before I reached the edge of the penalty area, I pushed the ball ahead and went.

"I realised immediately I had pushed it too far ahead. In that second I found myself in exactly the situation I had created thousands of times in practice to help me with my speed. The ball was going out. I had to stop it. It was wide of the goal and the goalkeeper did not know what was happening. The defender was nowhere. He thought it was going out. I got to it just before it crossed the line and hit it first time into the top corner of the net."

Five minutes later an almost identical situation arose. This time Mortensen reached the ball, controlled it and centred for Tommy Lawton to score.

Enough of the stories. What of the hard work which makes these dreams come true?

1. The Mortensen speed plan is an ideal practice for all players, particularly forwards. It calls for great determination.

2. Pressure Sprints: 50–70 yards, for pace, determination and stamina. From a standing start on the goal line, in groups of three and four, sprint to the half-way line and jog back gently. Groups should be made of runners of equal ability and must be given a proper start. If they are unequal, players will give up or start badly. In equal groups the competitive element produces good results. Do this once a week, with between ten and fourteen repetitions.

28

Over longer distances players should be encouraged to improve their breathing and powers of recovery by breathing excessively as well as correcting faulty running actions—too upright, splayed feet, poor arm action. Over short distances the emphasis must be not on pure running, but on thought and alertness.

A sprinter can concentrate entirely on the techniques of his running and win a race. A footballer must be able to think of other things while he is running—what he is going to do with the ball, how he is going to control it, where his other team players are. The quicker he can sum up a situation the more likely he is to arrive at the best spot first.

3. Ten–fifteen-yard sprints: these should be run in very small groups of any mixture. Make the players do something on the starting line which will partly take their minds off sprinting— like marking time, kneeling, lying down, leg cycling on their backs, standing on one leg, jumping. Combine this with a variety of "Go" commands—a shout, a whisper, a languid order. Use the same idea for backward running and turning. We do not work hard enough at turning in this country. By performing this practice with the starting-point between a wall and the finish line, the players can be called on to turn and change direction frequently.

4. Speed Reactions: these should be run over a very short distance, 8 to 10 yards, in pairs, with a start and a finish line. On the command "Go" the players, basically, sprint there and back. But in the course of this short run they must act on the coach's commands, "Turn" and run backwards, "Check", turn completely round, "Stop", pull up on the spot, "Jump", get up to an imaginary ball. This is a hard practice and physically demanding if done well. It punishes even harder the ground it is performed over, particularly in wet weather. Cinders or a durable surface are preferable to grass, not necessarily from the players' point of view but from the groundsman's.

5. Attacking the Ball: most match sprinting is done for the ball or to reach a position in which to receive the ball. Training should always introduce these principles.

A player standing on the 18-yard line faces another player on the half-way line who has a ball. When the ball is played firmly towards the first player he must sprint towards it, control it and pass it back accurately to the feeder before sprinting again to the half-way line. Vary the angle and nature of the pass. Cries of "Meet the ball!" always echo round a practice where professionals are at work. A lot of amateurs make their job harder by waiting for the ball to reach them. The quicker you get to a ball the longer you will have to do what you want with it.

Two or three players have their backs to a feeder who stands 20 yards away. As he plays the ball and shouts "Go" the players turn and compete for possession of the ball. That is, getting there and controlling it under pressure. This calls for speed, fast reactions and judgement. If the feeder plays the ball in the air or awkwardly, the player offering maximum speed and minimum thought often finds himself at a loss.

6. The Wall Game: a player with his back to a wall and only a short distance from it must turn and control the ball as it is kicked against the wall before it rebounds past him. The distance of the player from the wall can be varied according to his reflexes and ability.

7. Recovery and Drive:

i. Over a short distance: one player, or two players 5 yards apart, stand 10 yards off a line with their backs to it. Slightly in front of them a player with a ball stands facing the line. He must sprint between them with the ball and reach the line before they can turn and reach him. When he has succeeded once or twice, let the two players face the same way as the man with the ball.

ii. Over a longer distance: from some way out a player faces the goal with a ball at his feet. An opponent stands level with him or slightly behind him, facing the opposite direction. On "Go" the man in possession must sprint away with the ball and get a shot in. The opponent must try to catch him and stop him.

8. Overlap: running the length of the pitch together three players, A, B, and C, pass and interchange. B, in the middle, passes the ball to C, then immediately sprints behind and remains level with him on the other side. As he receives the ball C moves in towards the centre before passing to A, sprinting behind him into the overlap position. A, in the same way, moves into the centre with the ball.

As there is no competitive element this requires the backing of the coach. Although it is simple enough executed slowly, it requires thought and speed when done rapidly.

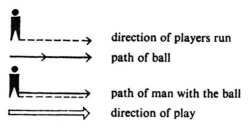

Key to Diagrams

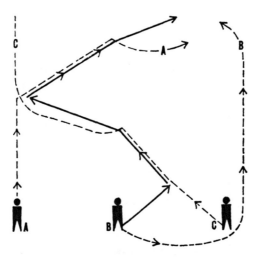

Fig. 1. Overlap sprinting and passing.

9. Anticipation: study almost any picture of a goalkeeper making a save against a team in which Denis Law is playing. Law will never be far from the goalkeeper unless, of course, he himself put the shot in from some way out. He has extremely fast reactions, but he earns himself a lot of goals by speed and anticipation. Time and again he will sprint at great speed to be on the spot when a goalkeeper makes a mistake or a half save. Brian Clough earned many of his forty goals a season this way. It requires an ability to read the game, determination—but, above all, sharpness. When the goalkeeper is under practice between the posts put one or two forwards on the edge of the penalty area to sprint in on him when he makes a save.

Change of pace is an art of deception which can be taught but is learned more successfully through experience. Wilf Mannion was one of its most skilful exponents. It requires judgement and ball control.

A defender in possession will frequently beat an attacker through simple change of pace because, too often, attackers rush in indiscriminately. For an attacker to beat his man with a change of pace is a more subtle skill which involves slowing down, luring the defender into a false sense of security and accelerating past him.

Beating a man in a dribble incorporates changing direction, sharply or subtly, or feinting to do so . . . and then changing pace. Too many players forget that without the sprint after a change of direction the advantage can easily be cancelled out by an alert defender. Watch the tremendous speed Bobby Charlton breaks into, just a stride or two after he has changed direction or gone past a player.

Stanley Matthews beat full-backs by first getting them off balance, or flat-footed, which is a skill in itself, then pushing the ball past them and accelerating at great pace after it. In all these short sprint practices Matthews would have emerged in front—and in the speed reaction test he would probably have been in a class on his own. Not only was he very fast. He was a great deal stronger than many realised.

The secret of using pure speed with the ball is knowing how far ahead you can play it with safety. A player like George Best travels easily with the ball, using change of pace, deception and fine ball control. When he beat Germano to score against Benfica in Manchester United's 5–1 win in Lisbon in the European Cup he merely took the ball up to the Portuguese and, when he committed himself, pushed it past him and took off after it at speed. Gento could run with the ball at great speed. But most players have to run after the ball.

The majority of players do not push the ball far enough ahead. Before they have accelerated into top speed they are forced to check to play the ball again, giving the defender an opportunity to get some sort of tackle in. Instead of pushing it three or four yards ahead, push it eight to ten yards past the man.

Eusebio, who is remarkably fast, pushes the ball a tremendous distance forward into an open space and is able to get there first.

On an individual run he will do this more than once, showing great acceleration. Peter Brabrook, of West Ham, although a seasoned First Division player, has improved on this technique lately. Mike Summerbee, of Manchester City, does this well and when he goes past a player he goes completely past him. Most of the best wingers do. The best I have ever seen was Harry Hooper as a young player with West Ham, but he seemed to lose that ability as he got older.

Held, the German World Cup player, can do it from anywhere on the field. He likes to get a well-balanced run of three or four yards at his opponent, push the ball past him either side, and go.

The first thing Tom Finney would do in a match was to kick the ball past his full-back and sprint after it to see how fast the full-back was on the turn. Finney was equally fast inside. He was a great player, in fact, and as Bill Shankly said of him when they played together, "If we were feeling tired in a match we gave the ball to Tom and asked him to dribble around for ten minutes."

Two tips: learn to control the ball with the outside of the foot for speed running with the ball. At the beginning of a sprint the ball can be pushed forward with the outside of the foot without interrupting the initial stride.

A great way of getting past a defence—the Germans try this a lot—is to kick the ball forward immediately it arrives, without controlling it, and sprinting after it. It is surprising how often it catches the defence static.

All great forwards are fast—Charlton, Suarez, Pele, Eusebio. The only one who springs to mind as not having a great speed was Puskas—but he had so many other highly developed skills. Above all, he showed what the others have in abundance, determination.

Determination in a trained player will often win him a short sprint. At one training session at Manchester City a sprinter who had recorded 9.7 seconds for the 100 yards came to give the players the once-over at our invitation. In a challenge over about 40 yards he gave Summerbee a yard start and two of the juniors, who are good runners, two yards start each. He was appalled when he lost to Summerbee by two yards and closed up only a yard on the two juniors. I should mention he was not in full training at the time. But even in the group running, over 50 and 60 yards, he was unable to sprint clear of any group, even the slowest. Over 100 yards he would almost certainly have been well ahead of the majority of the players. Here, competing against footballers' strength and determination—for many of them were technically poor runners—he had not done at all well. He and his coach were very surprised at the results. They said they could not understand why we did not win everything. I explained that there was a little more to football than that.

CHAPTER FIVE

Power and Technique

Anyone remotely connected with the game appreciates the player's need for a variety of ball skills, speed, agility. An alarming number of players and coaches refuse to acknowledge, or are simply ignorant of, the necessity of POWER.

The major difference between amateurs and professionals, the sixteen-year-old school boy in the first eleven and the sixteen-year-old apprentice professional, the amateur with excellent technique and the Fourth Division professional, is power. Of course there are differences in the levels of their skill also. But not as great as the disparity in power.

It is not difficult to see why. The professional devotes so much of his life to football activities that, however shallow his fitness is, he will derive one long-term effect from it all—extra strength. Even a professional not playing in the four Football League divisions has often had the advantage of a few years of full-time training. He will be able to exploit the effect of this strength of his physique even though his skill and fitness might have deteriorated.

Yet so few players at any level appreciate the value of power. Even less show any understanding of how it is produced. Amateurs, if they think about it at all, regard power as a class distinction. Professionals of some of the best clubs in the world imagine it will grow automatically. In many cases it will. But generally speaking footballers do not work hard enough at their strength. Even public demonstrations of it are seen with only half an eye.

When Eusebio places a ball for a free kick 40 yards out, every spectator knows he has enough power to put in a goal-scoring shot off a three- or four-pace run. When a forward like Charlton,

Pele or Puskas at his peak finds a chance to shoot, it is their extra power which vastly increases their potential danger.

Everyone, particularly First Division goalkeepers, knows about Bobby Charlton's shot. The same strength enables him to make an accurate 40 or 50 yard cross-field pass in full flight.

Tommy Lawton and Dixie Dean were legendary headers of the ball. Lawton's power in his neck and shoulders went almost unnoticed. He was classed simply as a player who was brilliant in the air.

Yet this is not a quality which appears from nowhere. Like everything else of lasting worth, it demands constant hard work, primarily in the form of repetitions, secondly through concentrated exercise.

When the Portuguese were training near Manchester during the World Cup, I watched their training routines quite regularly. After everyone had finished one player remained to carry on alone—Eusebio.

For thirty minutes he practised shooting from all distances, getting anyone to throw the balls back to him. He did this not because he had repetitions inprinted on his mind, but primarily because he enjoyed it. He knows how valuable the power of his shooting is to him and his team. He has demonstrated it on games. And it is a fair assumption he will have been through the same sort of schedule two or three times this week.

Sandor Kocsis—he was in the outstanding Hungarian side of the Puskas era before he played for Barcelona—was one of the greatest headers the game has ever seen. The dedication he showed in developing and maintaining that talent shows just why he was so good.

For hours and hours he would get anyone to supply him with crosses to head. Each week he averaged three or four hundred practice crosses headed into the net. The size of his neck muscles proved what this was doing for him. The number of headed goals he scored proved to him and to many others that power with technique is unstoppable. And repetitions are a requisite for both.

When Tommy Lawton was a boy of fifteen at Burnley he spent hours of his spare time leaping to head a ball swinging on a rope from a girder. He did this, he says, until his forehead was red-raw. His ability to climb to a high ball was based on timing.

What he did when he was up there was based on power. All of it was based on practice.

The more spectacular results of repetitive practice show themselves frequently. Pele, even during the World Cup in England when he was restricted by some serious knocks, often did more training than the rest of the Brazilians. Once again it was his shooting and kicking he chose to concentrate on, although he ran and sprinted a lot on his own.

In repetition skills players are more likely to enjoy something they are good at. If you like hitting centres over to the far corner of the goal area with your right foot, or aiming to drop goal kicks just over the centre circle, or shooting, when you are asked to do it ten times it is easy. Twenty times is acceptable. Fifty times has something tedious about it. If it is something you are not good at, such repetition rapidly develops into a painful bore.

But it must be done. There is no way round it. To develop the explosive strength in a particular technique which might be called on only two or three times in a match, the movement must have been practised hundreds and hundreds of times beforehand.

This is a necessity in any sport. Gary Player and Jack Nicklaus do not hit a golf ball further than other golfers simply because they are better players. Their power is greater than most other professionals who have just the same opportunities.

Both men force themselves through the routine drudgery of repetition. Either of them will hit 500, 600 practice balls a day as a natural exercise. Gary Player, who is a small man, frequently hits 300 practice balls before playing 18 holes—on a quiet day before a big tournament. And all for something he said was "a cissy game" before he played it at the age of fifteen.

Of course it is much easier for a recognised sportsman. The fruits of Player's success bring him equipment, a range, assistants and time, all of which are the servants of his dedication. But it was the dedication which brought him all this. I can make it easier for the fifteen- and sixteen-year-old boys I coach. In ten minutes, at any time of the day or night, I can put them through repetitions exercises which will leave them gasping. The facilities are there for them. One of my jobs is to get the best out of them —the facilities and the players.

Scores of disadvantages make things harder for 90 per cent of others with ambitions in the game. No nets, no lights, poor pitch, not enough balls. Sometimes nobody to practise with. Jimmy McIlroy and Alfredo Di Stefano were two of many great players who remembered the lonely practice they put in "when the others had gone home because they had had enough".

The basic repetitions I use are NOT an addition to training at the end of the day. They are one of the hardest parts of any player's schedule and make the ninety minutes of a match seem like an afternoon in the garden. The success of anything strenuous and difficult depends on two things: the ability of the coach to sustain the practice and drive the players when he is tired and things are not going well: and the mental courage of the player to keep trying and concentrating when his legs or neck muscles are aching to go their own way.

The essential repetitions are these: heading into goal, shooting, defensive clearances.

The maximum number to aim for is 400 in a week, split between two sessions. For a professional this is a hard morning's work, probably two hours of exacting individual effort with brief intervals when the coach makes a point on technique.

For amateurs this number should be varied according to the strength of the players. Age means less than strength as far as this is concerned, although obviously a team of twelve- and thirteen-year-olds could not be expected to reach a figure as high as 400. At the same time individuals of a similar age group will not have an identical maximum. Don't make it too easy. Remember this is not a test of strength. It is a development of it.

The practice should always be governed by the number of repetitions to be reached, not the length of time to be spent on it. If a player is to work on heading in 200 crosses, his performance will ebb and flow between 0–10 and 8–10 on target. Certainly he will get tired, very tired. But he will work better with crosses on his mind rather than the clock. Restricting the practice to, say 45 minutes, often works to the disadvantage of the player if the crosses are bad or he keeps shooting into the middle distance. The temptation after thirty-five minutes when he is tired and all the balls have disappeared is to say: "That will do." And that will definitely not do. For, because he is weak he is doing less. He should be doing more.

Needed in all these practices: One or two players crossing balls into the goalmouth, a goalkeeper (not essential), a ball boy or two unless there are a large number of balls available, and a target (a goal).

The players crossing the ball should be those who would benefit from doing so—and that means almost anyone, even a goalkeeper.

The goalkeeper should be restricted to staying close to his line. By cutting out centres he will distract the player who is the centre-piece of the practice. His heading is under pressure, nothing else.

The coach plays a vital role in these practices. When the player is doing well he needs to say nothing. When his efficiency begins to deteriorate the coach must squeeze extra effort and concentration out of the player by goading, bullying, chastising, encouraging him, anything to make him work harder.

1. Heading in crosses: the player has one object—to get the ball into the goal with his head, whatever the cross.

He will discover a number of things without being told—that he has a better chance of hitting the target by heading back to the far post than by trying to turn the ball—and it is easier too; that taking his eye off the ball when he is tired means he is more likely to head it badly and uncomfortably.

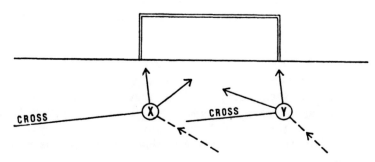

Fig. 2. Heading crosses: X for deflection, Y for heading back.

2. Shooting: all the great goal scorers—Greaves, Eusebio, Law, Sivori, Pele and Hurst—hit the ball quickly, not necessarily as hard as they can, but with power. This repetition shooting practice is to develop power and ability in first-time shooting. The majority of scoring chances come in the air, or bouncing, or if they are running along the ground the ball will arrive

fast and awkwardly. However the ball comes, it will very seldom arrive in any way like it arrived in the five-minute pre-match period which everyone seems to regard as shooting-in practice. The object is for the player to get a shot in first time. No control, just hit it. The inconsistency of the crosses, particularly if feeders are asked to vary them, will mean that balls will be coming at the pressured player in an assortment of ways.

Once again he will pick up points of technique instinctively—the importance of balance, which foot is best for balls from different sides and angles, how often he can expect success from just hitting a ball without aiming.

3. Defenders' clearances: every defender must be able to kick a ball clear, first time, from his own penalty area. He must have the power to reach a safe area, usually the wings.

The same basic principles are involved in this practice. As the crosses, in any form, are fed to the defender he must have a target to aim for—anyone he can find with the ball and who will return it.

It is imperative that all players put under this form of repetitive pressure should have a target to aim for. Every player should get either the feeling of satisfaction of success or inadequacy of failure.

4. Defenders' headed clearances: exactly the same practice is involved. The crosses should all be in the air, of course, and the target not so far away.

All these practices can be modified successfully for three players. If there are only two it becomes more difficult unless they can lay their hands on a large supply of balls. But two can still benefit. One serves, the other heads back. One lobs or chips, the other drives it back at him. The disadvantage here is that both players tire at the same time and the value is reduced immediately.

One player practising on his own is limited. A wall is his only aid. This is a wonderful way of developing individual skill and technique, and, over a period of time, power.

I have put a lot of stress on power and its general neglect—and I have not finished yet. If it is so important, and I am convinced it is, practices for power need organisation, supervision and time.

CHAPTER SIX

Power and Physique

Time is everyone's enemy in this game. A footballer can expect to play only a certain number of years. In many of these years he will be on the way down. Amateurs can expect to find only limited periods of free time for training. As he gets older time gets dearer. Unless a player is a professional he will never have more time for training than when he is at school or university.

Already I have outlined practices which for results depend on constant use. From many of them comes fitness through practice. But we have still to deal with the fundamental basis of power and strength—exercise.

In the three categories into which my coaching and training schedules are divided, calisthenics or free exercises—the simple body exercises of physical training—plays no part whatsoever. If that kind of training is to be of any value the exercises need to be repeated so often there is little time left for anything else. For an amateur this is ridiculous. For a professional it is uneconomic and boring.

Except for the goalkeeper, free exercises have a usefulness in football for warming up and suppleness, but little more than that. Nobody gets fit by doing morning breathing exercises by the open window. This is merely a routine which offsets some of the harm poor living does to the system. It cannot be bad. But it is not good enough. Free exercises in football involve the same principle.

Players for whom I have complete responsibility divide their training time into three categories—skills and playing football, running, and weight exercises. The last of these demands the least time but the most effort.

The veil of mysticism which seems to surround weight training for footballers has never been swept aside by even the leading professional clubs. Probably about ten clubs use weights properly. A few dabble at them. The rest dismiss weights as objects that are used by the vain to get body bulk that is never used and by the injured to build up muscles that have wasted away.

I am not going to waste time destroying any ill-founded arguments or ridiculing the misuse of weights for the cult of the body beautiful.

The word weights alone strikes doubt and even fear in many footballers' minds. All I ask is that the doubters should listen to the opinion of anyone who has used weights seriously in the search for extra power. Do not make a decision based on ignorance.

The clearest evidence of the success of weight training is in athletics, where it is a recognised part of almost every individual's programme.

World records are falling everywhere. This year athletes are jumping higher, running faster and throwing further than they did last year, not only at international levels but at smaller meetings. Is anyone certain that weight training can take the credit? Of course not. But there is no doubt that well-executed weight exercises are the best known way of gaining strength and power —not skill, but the foundation upon which skill is built.

And it was proved a long, long time ago that you do not get a hernia every time you pick up a heavy weight, or become musclebound, or slow up, if you lift weights regularly.

Ignorance courts danger. An expert's opinion and instruction is advisable if you are going to use weights . . . firstly on the equipment needed, secondly on the safety rules equipment demands, thirdly how to use it. All this can be done comfortably in half a dozen sessions. Usually the nearest athletic club is the easiest place to find people with experience of weight-lifting for speed and power.

I have experimented with weights since my early days at West Ham, and used them at every club I have been with. The advice I work under is from Ron Pickering, the AAA's national coach, who has a specific interest in weights for power in all sports.

I use, basically, five exercises for players ranging from the ages of twelve and thirteen to well over thirty.

The exercises are elementary and uncomplicated. This does

not make them any easier to do. All are common knowledge. Long-jumper Lynn Davies, coached by Ron Pickering, used these same exercises in the build-up towards his leap of 26 ft. 5¾ in. which won him a gold medal in Tokyo. Davies, of course, is an athlete of the highest quality whose ability is not limited to long-jumping and sprinting. Weights on their own do not account for his success. But his achievements, and others whom Ron Pickering has trained in a similar way, point to the obvious conclusion that he and his coach are working on the right lines.

So let's try it.

Safety Rules

1. Check that the collars are tight on the barbell and that weights are secure.

2. Spotters must be standing by, ready to take the weight when lifting heavy poundages.

3. Treat the subject seriously.

4. All lifts must be performed with a straight, flat back—never with a rounded back.

5. Heels must remain in contact with the ground at all times, except in the calf-raising exercise.

Light weights

The exercises I am going to describe performed with a light weight are useful for muscular endurance. But using heavy weights in short concentrated effort is the best way of improving power.

Amount of weights

This is impossible to prescribe. It is related primarily to the body weight of the lifter and then his confidence in his ability.

Age

I have used heavy weights for power with schoolboys of twelve and thirteen years of age, safely and successfully. Players of this age often accept the idea more enthusiastically than the seasoned professional, educated on less controversial matter. I believe weights can be used at an even younger age, but I don't know. One of my sons who is seven enjoys doing the free exercises he learns at school holding small five-pound dumbells. He is naturally quite a strong boy and the weights give him confidence. But enjoyment is the key-note, not strength.

Confidence

Players have to accustom themselves to the idea and to the feel of the weights. This is where the competent initial instruction from someone who knows what he is doing is important.

Warming up

Never do anything from a cold start, least of all weights. With professionals I do sprints, between 10 to 50 yards, immediately before weights . . . never the reverse.

The exercises (see photographs facing pages 112 and 113)

1. The Clean: the bar is pulled from ground to shoulder height in one movement, beginning with the legs and followed by the trunk and arms. There are no complicated movements like splitting or squatting under the bar. But this could become a natural development.

2. The Squat: the bar is held across the shoulders with the back kept erect. The lifter squats until either the weights reach the lower limit of the safety rack (as on the photograph) or until his seat touches a firm bench or seat. He then returns to the upright position.

3. The Step-up: the bar is held across the shoulders in the same way as in the previous exercises (the squat). The lifter steps up on to a 14–16-in. high bench to stand erect and then steps down again.

4. The Bench-press: the lifter lies along a bench, with his feet flat on the ground and lifts the weights above his chest.

5. The Calf-raiser: the weights rest on the shoulders again and the lifter comes on to his toes, down on to his heels and up again.

Breathing

In the early lessons it is imperative for a coach to be present to ensure the correct breathing. Basically, you breathe IN as you prepare for the effort, OUT at the explosion of effort. Breathe excessively. The oxygen burned making the effort has to be replenished. Being out of breath means there is too much air in the lungs and not enough oxygen. Breathing hard dispels the stale air and generates more oxygen. Gordon Pirie was probably the most obvious example of an athlete who breathed excessively during the effort of a race to dispel air and create oxygen.

Routine of the exercises

A player's strength will vary day by day. Whatever exercise he is doing must be completed correctly. He should be allowed to remain on the same weight for two, three or even four sessions. Increases should be slight. He should perform the exercise in repetitions of three as a minimum, increasing to eight before going on to a heavier weight at the next session. Then rest. The ultimate object is that the player should have to make a tremendous effort at some stage to complete the exercise he is engaged in. If he cannot do it the weights must be lowered until he can. Remember it is not the weights that are doing the good, it is the exercise. Never go on lifting if the exercise is being done badly.

Weight increases

A young player will normally make rapid progress until he begins to near his maximum for that particular exercise. Older players do not make such fast progress, but this does not necessarily diminish the value. Here is a rough guide. Everything depends on how often the weights are used. If it is once a week then this chart will apply; if it is twice a week, as I do with professionals, progress will obviously be faster.

	Beginners	*After 6 months*	*After 12 months*
Clean	¾ body weight	body weight	1¼ body weight
Squat	body weight	1½ body weight	twice body weight
Step-up	¾ body weight	body weight	1½ body weight
Bench-press	½ body weight	¾ body weight	body weight
Calf raiser	½ body weight	¾ body weight	body weight

At Manchester City there are sixteen-year-old juniors, weighing only 9 stone, who can lift 260 lb. What pleases me more is that they are strong enough to play in middle of the field positions in the Central League. And League reserve team football is physically very demanding.

It is not easy to gauge progress in the sort of strength football demands. Here are two improvement tests to see how body power will increase.

Standing Long Jump: stand behind a line with your toes just touching it and feet slightly apart. Spring forward as far as possible, making a mark where the heels land. You may bend the legs and swing the arms before jumping, but preliminary jumps are not allowed.

Performance rating:
    Any distance below one's own height: poor.
    Own standing height: below average.
    Six inches beyond standing height: average.
    Twelve inches beyond standing height: good.
    Twenty-four inches beyond standing height: very good.
    Thirty-six inches beyond standing height: excellent.

The world record is 11 ft. 7 in. Lynn Davies (who is 6 ft. tall) can do 10 ft. 2 in.; Mike Summerbee (5 ft. 11 in. tall), 9 ft. 5 in.; Alan Oakes (5 ft. 11 in. tall), 8 ft. 10 in.; Tony Book (5 ft. 9 in. tall), 8 ft. 7 in.

Vertical Jump: stand facing a blank wall with both arms full stretched above your head, keeping the heels on the ground. Get someone to make a chalk mark on the wall at full reach of the finger-tips. Turn sideways to the wall. Take a piece of chalk in one hand and leap vertically, marking the wall with the chalk as high as possible. Measure the difference in inches between the two marks.

Performance rating:
    Ten inches—poor; 14 in.—below average; 18 in.—average; 22 in.—good; 26 in.—very good; over 30 in.—excellent.
    Arthur Rowe (17 stone) has achieved 31 in.; Lynn Davies, 32 in.; Valeriy Brumel, 40 in.; Wynn Davies (Newcastle), 22 in.

These are two simple tests of leg explosive power. In football the legs do most of the work, the knees take most of the pressure and the ankles take most of the knocks.

Years ago, even in sprinting, the top half of the body was regarded as relatively unimportant and having no real influence on performance. Sprinters were nearly always slim and sparse.

The theory was that this sort of build "cut down wind resistance".

On the track, ideas have progressed rapidly, often dramatically. The upper half of the body is now accepted as very much a driving force. Look at the build of the modern class of sprinters like Bob Hayes, who has the physique of a boxer.

Weight exercises to strengthen the upper part of the body have come to be an essential part of most sprinters' training. And this for a sport which has no body contact.

Once again football is lagging years behind. Strength and power is not exclusively a question of being able to shoot from 30 yards or of being as fast off the mark as a sprinter. It is a thousand things more—the intensively competitive hustle and bustle of any game, tackling, holding off a tackle, getting in a shot or a pass under pressure, taking knocks, recovering from injuries, reaching the ball first, getting up to the ball in a ruck of players and activity, doing with a wet ball what you can do with a dry one, lasting the whole 90 minutes . . . and so on.

Here is the value of body strength—power from head to toe. Yet it is almost incomprehensible that Lynn Davies does more work with the top half of his body in a week, mostly in his own time, than many professional footballers do in a season.

John Charles, I consider, not only had a footballer's ideal build but used it correctly. His press nickname of the "Gentle Giant" was rather misleading. It gave the impression that he plodded about the field being pleasant to everyone. In fact, he never used his powers unfairly. Once or twice in Italy, when he was asked physically to "take care of" an opponent, he refused. I could never picture this man of 6 ft. 2 in., 14 stone, with a 46 inch chest, being gentle when it came to quick shooting or passing, or leaping to a cross in the penalty area when he was often heavily marked and impeded.

It is impossible to develop the upper part of the body simply playing football. The weight exercises I have prescribed make it possible for you to develop almost every part of the body.

The emphasis should always be on leg power. To neglect the rest of the body is to reduce the value of weights and the benefit of extra strength. If the five exercises are done correctly, the top half of the body will get the attention it needs.

It has taken a lot of words and time to explain part of what I

47

feel about weights. One of their great advantages is that they demand so little of a player's practice time. A class of a dozen can complete the whole schedule of exercises in twenty minutes or half an hour. For an amateur, particularly, this must be one of their greatest attractions.

What results can you expect? Do not misinterpret the rewards of weight training. Many players, amateurs more than professionals, who have dabbled with weights use them as a substitute for training. This is almost entirely useless. Weight training will make a player stronger, but it will not turn a seventeen-year-old who cannot cross a ball into someone with a shot like Bobby Charlton's. It will make everyone a better jumper, quicker getting to the ball. But it will make nobody a better header or kicker unless he practises the techniques of kicking and heading at the same time.

Strength through weights is the source of a quality that every level of the game demands, a quality which is too often overlooked—confidence.

So many aspects of football are intangible. Arithmetical assessment of skills and ability is difficult. Strength and confidence are very closely related, of that I am certain. A young player who has proved to himself that his strength is improving, that today he is lifting a certain number of pounds which last week he could not manage, is bursting with confidence in his strength.

And here is the basis of determination and courage. When two players are equal in ability the stronger will win. If they are unequal and it is the stronger who has more ability he will certainly win. Even if he has less ability he might win because he will feel confident in his strength. Of course, there is a great deal more to winning games than this alone. When the game is reduced to an individual contest, however, man against man, in a sprint for the ball, a tackle, a header, this is when it counts most.

If a telegram dropped on any amateur's doormat tomorrow ordering him to play in a First Division League match that same evening, I guarantee the first panic reaction would be: 'I don't feel up to it. I am not strong enough or fit enough to last ninety minutes." And his legs would feel weak, not entirely through nerves. Lack of ability is only the secondary consideration. Extra strength would produce more confidence although, on ability alone, he might never have the remotest chance of getting in the game.

If a coach can get an individual footballer to play to 90 per cent of his ability he is doing extremely well. Without confidence, a player's maximum performance could be reduced to 40 per cent of his ability, or even less.

At the professional level a player without confidence knows his chances of recapturing that lost percentage of his ability during a game is small.

At an amateur level, where the course of the game is influenced more by mistakes, his chances are higher. So too is the possibility of hiding a weakness.

In each case, however, neither player will be able to impose his will or ability on the game or on his opponent. Strength might restore his confidence in his ability. It might not. But it will give him something to hang on to.

Strength is no substitute for ability any more than weights are a substitute for ball practice. Mistakenly, though, strength is the least considered essential at all levels. From it comes not only the ability to dominate, but the more important capacity to exploit talent to the utmost degree through possessing the power to do it and the confidence to want to do it.

This is the great value of weight training . . . . a remarkable return for little time spent.

Bobby Moore worked extremely hard on his strength when he was a boy at Upton Park. Probably the most startling development came from Norman Piper, the Plymouth Argyle player. He always had ample ability but was never strong enough to bring it into the game—and these were junior and reserve games.

For six months he worked hard on weights, beginning with a very low poundage. He was sixteen then, and as a boy of only 9 st. 5 lb. and 5 ft. 6 in. tall had everything against him physically. Because he was small he was classed as an outside-right and at that age most managers and guardians would have been content to feed him well, ensure he had plenty of early nights, and hope for the best. But if a player is willing to work, and he also has ability, there is hardly any limit to the speed of his progress.

On his seventeenth birthday he played in the club's first team. By then he was squatting with 300 lb. and pressing 140 lb. Now he is a talented mid-field worker with considerable potential. Blackpool wanted him as the replacement for Alan Ball when he was transferred to Everton.

It was Piper's new strength which he had won by lonely application and sweat that brought him to the top. He has played for England Youth and I am sure he has years of top-class football in him.

It is a frustrating thought that thousands of players are not giving their best because they lack one quality which is well within their grasp. Don't be one of them.

CHAPTER SEVEN

Balance

Any group of footballers will include at least one whom people will term "a natural player", in the sense that he picks up skills easily, looks comfortable with the ball, and often manages to do the right thing by instinct. But, however psychologists care to analyse it, soccer is fundamentally an unnatural game. In an unnatural game involving a great deal of staccato movement, a variety of running and plenty of body contact, the division between a good player and a bad one has much to do with balance.

Football is complicated by theorists who contribute nothing but words. Some mean well. Others are nothing more than imposters. It is not my job to theorise unless I can produce some practical results. Here, there is a danger of making a point and leaving it up in the clouds instead of bringing it down to earth. Balance is not the sort of technique which is written into a schedule somewhere between sprints and pressure heading. It is, however, a quality of which players should be aware and which coaches should appreciate increases the efficiency of a player's skill.

Poor balance is easy enough to recognise. Small children fall about for two reasons—they enjoy it, and it is easier than standing up. Compare a professional and an amateur match and see how often amateurs fall down and stumble in contrast to the professionals. Ungainly players often retain their balance when a situation demands some sort of action or change of direction by doing the next easiest thing to sitting down—careering on in a straight line or standing rooted to the ground.

Football, of course, produces scores of off-balance situations —the time factor, emergencies, the very unnaturalness of the game, contribute to this. Frequently it is the poorly balanced player who makes an emergency out of every situation.

Eradicating poor balance is not so straightforward. An elementary mistake less gifted players fall into is trying to do something too far away from the ball, rather like a golfer or a tennis player swinging at the ball standing too far away from it. Most professionals have never been corrected about balance. The good ones, by instinct, get to a situation quickly and take the ball, trap it or head it in the most comfortable way by having their bodies ready early. An amateur will often take more time deciding what to do, move less quickly and consequently find himself under pressure to perform even the simplest skill.

Watch an experienced mid-field player turn with the ball. His body is already partly turned before he and the ball meet.

The first rules, then, are: get right on top of the situation; adjust the body before the ball arrives, not as it arrives.

Telling players to stop falling over sounds about as wise as telling wayward forwards to stop shooting wide. There is a little more to it than that. Players who are on the ground a lot—whether it is after going up for a ball, tackling or clearing—are usually poor players. Many do it because their technique is ill-timed and off-balance. Others do it out of bad habit, not necessarily lack of co-ordination but lack of thought.

A player on the ground is out of the game. He should be made to realise this. He should consciously make an effort not to fall over. If necessary he should readjust the way he performs a particular skill to help him keep his balance.

Constant practice through repetitions and under pressure will help a player's balance. Where a skill is weak, balance will almost certainly be poor—but it is sometimes a problem to distinguish cause from effect. Most players, for example, find it easier to balance on the opposite leg to the one which is used most for kicking. Practice with a small, lively ball in situations similar to a playground game are good for balance. And footballers brought up in the hard school of playground football have usually learned the necessity of remaining on their feet.

One particular practice involving another of the game's complications will help players' balance. In a rectangle 10 yards long and 5 yards wide about seven defenders cover the area between them. From a short distance three players, each with a ball under control, try to move into the defended area and out the other side. It demands control, bravery and balance to get through.

Cassius Clay, despite his 6 ft. 3 in. and 215 lb. fighting weight, is a superbly balanced athlete. As his weight increased from the time he won the Olympic title at the age of seventeen his sense of balance never wavered for two reasons—the practice he put in and the power he built. To be poised for quick movement in any direction, ready to duck or weave and throw the heaviest possible punch, demands great power and fitness in the legs. He is on his toes every second ready to commit himself or to avoid being committed.

A footballer should aim for the same skill—particularly defenders. Commitment, a full-back diving into a tackle, is less exhausting than hovering, jockeying, correcting and readjusting the body waiting for the good chance.

Similarly, if a player is to be able to get to a ball quicker to give him time to adjust his body, he needs to be faster. There is no doubt that fitness and power are more than half the battle in improving balance.

Big men are not necessarily less well-balanced than small men. John Charles, with a similar build to Cassius Clay, was equally well balanced. Neil Young (Manchester City) and Derek Dougan (Wolves) are two forwards who are both over 6 feet tall but have fine balance. So have the great kickers in the game like Eusebio, Charlton, Kubala and Puskas. The real test is icy grounds, when small steps can make things easier. Generally, long-striding players seem to lack something in balance in most conditions, although Peter Osgood of Chelsea is an outstanding example of a tall, long-striding player who combines this with excellent balance.

The player with the most improved balance is undoubtedly Geoff Hurst of West Ham. As a wing-half he was good, strong but not exceptional. In two years as a forward he had adjusted his game so that now he is as strong as ever. Vastly improved balance and confidence have given him the poise of class. The best example was in the World Cup semi-final against Portugal when he created Bobby Charlton's second goal. Hurst was competing for the ball with a Portuguese defender who was slightly between him and the goal. He managed to reach the ball at speed, control it and turn instantly, leaving the defender out of the game. It was a simple job to roll it back into Charlton's path.

CHAPTER EIGHT

Skill—Kicking

Skill, like intelligence, is not necessarily governed by age. Although there is a limit to both in every individual, skill is much more a reward for hard work down below than a gift from up above.

It would be simpler to catalogue players by age groups for practices. But skill does not improve, nor is it judged, by age. In professional football seventeen-year-olds compete with the over 30s; in schoolboy football a fifteen-year-old often appears in an under-18 team and a seven-year-old can look years ahead of an eight-year-old who has only just started playing the game.

The two qualities which dictate the degree of skill and the sort of practice a player should be made to attempt are strength and experience. I can remember trying to rectify identical faults —it happened to be scooping the ball with the weaker foot— in an eight-year-old, a thirteen-year-old schoolboy, a Cambridge University student and a Central League professional. Their needs and attitudes differed considerably. So did their strength. This was what dictated the speed they learned the skill and the way I taught it.

The range I want to cover in these skills practices is from nil to professional level. Within that range players seem to divide themselves into roughly four levels for each particular skill.

1. Digesting the basic ideas and enjoying doing it often for its own sake.

2. Forming some instinctive habits and using them when there is time competitively and in games where strength is often uneven.

3. The standard where strength is roughly level and skill alone determines whether a player is good enough to overcome dis-

tractions like physical contact, close marking, tension and excitement.

4. The stage where the skill becomes almost incidental to the game, usually the professional level. In practice great pressure can be put on the players, forcing them to unrecognized limits and giving them the ability to think two or three moves ahead.

An example of this: Tommy Lawton, going up to head a ball, could judge the flight of the ball, time his run, jump, take his eye off the ball, picture what the goalkeeper was doing, pick up the ball in flight again and head it where the goalkeeper wasn't . . . all under pressure.

I have not delved into the depths of theory behind each skill. This is a practical book and I regard the theory of skills like grammar and the structure of the language to someone learning French—it is essential to know the basic points, but the best way of learning is by getting out and trying it. Leave the technicalities to the academics and professionals.

Movement must be brought in as soon as possible, whatever skill is being practised. Performing a skill standing still is like learning a language without speaking it. Movement lends the beginnings of realism.

Regardless of how he performs a skill in practice, a player should be judged at one time only—in the competition of a match. Coaches fall into this trap less than players who, for example, often feel that because they can hit a ball with both feet in practice they are two-footed footballers. If they could see themselves in a match they would realise that under pressure they were hopelessly one-footed and about as one-eyed as Cyclops—and equally as ungainly.

Of all the causes of this poor showing in a game, the two most common are distractions and sheer lack of practice. And in the long run it will all come down to practice. I do not for one minute believe that all the great players began their playing days with rotten potatoes, stuffed pincushions and knotted rags, as their memoirs would have us believe, because they could not afford a ball. But I do know that many of them achieved success only after spending a vast amount of time with a ball. Mastery is essential, perfection the ideal. And whatever space is devoted to skills here or in any other book or in organised practice, this is no indication of the time that must be spent on ball work.

55

"No, I can't really remember practising in my spare time," said Pele. "It's easier to remember the times I didn't practise. And most of those were when I was watching."

And Eusebio: "I was introduced to a ball at an early age," he once said. "We seemed to take a liking to each other and we have hardly ever been apart since."

The influence of example is a strong one in football. Helenio Herrara, the Inter-Milan coach, told me that he bought Suarez for £197,000 from Barcelona for two reasons—firstly, he is Europe's best creative inside-forward, and secondly, he puts tremendous effort into his training, leads the other players and sets a high example of skill.

For the outsider, professional football offers some good examples. In each section I shall give a list of players in the game at the moment who perform the skill well, often brilliantly. A less skilled player can learn by watching a good professional. Of course, too many younger players tend to copy the gestures, the extravagances of professionals. The skills slip by unnoticed.

So let's get on with some work.

If a coach or a player is ever in doubt about what to practise he will never be wrong if he chooses kicking. The gulf between professionals and amateurs in this skill is a gaping one. Professionals club the ball. The contact makes a different noise from what is heard in most other games. Poor technique in kicking makes a hash of good intention. And kicking is really what the game is all about.

The ability to kick a long way is vital and under-estimated. If a player cannot kick distances he is forced to play it short. The best players look for the far man first. If a pass is not possible, he will bring his sights down. Hundreds of players are forced to play at point-blank range for ever. Accuracy comes somewhere along the line of distance . . . depending, like everything else, on the amount of practice.

The basic rules: the position of the head regulates, first, where the non-kicking foot will go and, secondly, because of that, where the ball will go. So the head has it. If it is OVER the ball it will keep low. If it is BEHIND the ball it will go up. If it is to the side the tendency will be to swing at the ball with a straightish leg and the non-kicking foot will be well away from the ball. The result is a scoop. Many players do this with their weaker foot, but it is a dangerous habit. Driving the ball straight will become very difficult, kicking with the outside of the foot impossible. Players should concentrate on kicking straight with a back-swing and follow through like a cricketer.

A footballer's leg and foot should be like a golf club with an adjustable head. At the moment of contact the leg and foot are locked, not flapping like a small child's learning to kick.

Practices: there is nothing more boring than kicking in pairs. Threes are better, with a man in the middle. This cuts down the time wasted when the ball is miskicked. In all the early practices introduce the same progressions—standing still, movement from side to side and forwards to meet the ball—before increasing distance. Start with:

1. The inside of the foot—it is the easiest way to begin, using the widest part of the foot. It is almost impossible not to put the non-kicking foot next to the ball.

2. Instep—remember the basic principles of the head and the line. Lack of confidence and strength encourages swinging at the ball.

3. Outside of the foot—watch for distribution of weight.

Do the same sequence with the other foot; now vary it, making the player change feet. Speed it up. A player will soon realise that kicking with the inside of the foot calls for quick adjustment; the outside of the foot for less adjustment.

Increase distance but keep as much movement as possible in the practice.

This is all very simple, some players will feel. Yet however many years they have been playing their kicking can always be improved, often by going back to square one. Just to prove how low the standard of kicking is, try these tests which can be made into team competitions.

The object: to kick the ball so that it hits the back of the net without touching the ground; no goalkeeper; a still ball.

From: the penalty spot, the penalty area arc, both corners of the penalty area, 25 yards, 35 yards, the edge of the penalty area on the goal line.

Vary the feet. Try it first with a dead ball, then with a moving ball. Also with a faster moving ball—from distances between 10 yards and 30 yards—how many players are good enough to get six out of six into the goal? Very few, even from the shortest distances. How many can kick over the bar with either foot from the edge of the area? Or get the ball between the posts from the half-way line?

Judgement is half the battle in kicking—being able to estimate the power needed to land the ball on the spot from corners, free kicks, goal kicks and moving ball situations above all. Poor judgement is demonstrated as often as poor technique in amateur games.

Long kicking and control competition: this is played between two target areas—the centre circle and part of the penalty area defined by producing imaginary lines from the goal area to the

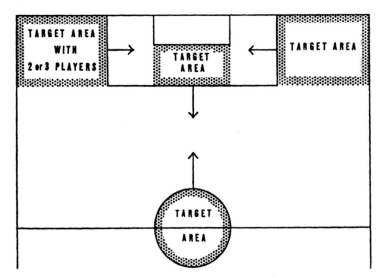

Fig. 3. Long kicking and control.

18-yard line; or from one corner to another. One or two players in each area; with a dead ball the flighted kick from one area must be aimed to drop into the other area; the opponent must control the ball on the volley, anyhow, and keep it up for two touches before trapping and placing it for his dead ball kick. Failure to control or hit the target area, concede one point to the opposition. The first to score 20 wins. Change at 10 because the areas are deliberately unequal and varied in shape.

Conditioned games practices:

1. 15-yard kicking only; weaker foot only.

2. For long kicking out of defence: each side plays with six defenders and four forwards. Once the game has started the defenders must not cross the half-way line nor the forwards recross it. It means defenders clearing the ball are forced to kick long to reach their four forwards in the other half. This condition also encourages forwards, who are outnumbered, to run off the ball. By alternating the forward/defender ratio more or less pressure can be put on defenders.

3. Clearing, shooting and fitness: five defenders and a goalkeeper are confined to the penalty area. Five forwards have a limited time, say five minutes, to score as many goals as possible. If the defenders win the ball they can touch it only twice between them. They gain their only respite by clearing the ball as far as possible upfield. If the ball crosses the touchline, however, the attackers are awarded a penalty. To make forwards shoot from a distance, restrict them to outside the penalty area.

4. First time kicking: a goal is needed, makeshift or conventional, with playing space in front and behind; a goalkeeper. Two players each side of the goal work together to score the goals. Individually, one touch only; combined, only two touches either side of the goal. It will work out that one player will set up a shot for one of the others. The ball will drive them back and angled kicking, chipping and shooting will introduce itself.

Examples of some good kickers in the game today: Herd, Hurst, Moore, Peters, Harris, Elder, Angus, Baxter, Haynes, Smith (Liverpool), Brown (Everton), Summerbee, Charlton, Fantham, Lorimer and Law.

The ultimate to aim for is Eusebio's standard. He has developed the technique of putting the non-kicking foot in front of the ball. This means he is virtually kicking into the ground, but it ensures that the ball keeps low for a maximum distance. So, with his immense power, he can shoot from 40 yards and the ball, instead of rising as it does when others try the same thing, will remain low enough to have a chance of scoring.

On the other hand, Jimmy Greaves shoots with speed and accuracy under pressure through being able to adjust his body rapidly, and restrict the back-swing of his leg.

It all comes from skill, practice and power—and plenty of all three.

CHAPTER NINE

Skill—Heading

Heading is, on the face of it, unnatural. A beginner's first re-action is one of fear—fear of getting the ball on the face, prob-ably. A coach's job should be to build skill through confidence, not through pain. There is no avoiding the issue—a player gets hurt if he heads badly. The thing to impress on a young player is that whoever designed the skull must have been a keen foot-baller. For the forehead is so thick it appears to have been made exclusively for heading a football. And the only way to ensure heading in the correct place is by keeping the eyes open.

These are briefly the stages of progression, with the feeder, usually another player, throwing the ball each time.

1. From a short distance the player heads the ball back to the feeder.

2. Then he heads it down to him.

3. Then the ball is thrown to either side of the player and he must move to reach it and head it back. This is the beginning of a challenge between him and the ball.

4. Then he heads it down.

Now increase the distance and height to bring in judgement, progressing through the same four stages.

It won't take long to reach this point. By then the obstacle of fear will be crumbling. The spadework of confidence has been done. Now build on it.

Go through the routine of the four stages again, but now the player must hit it back to the thrower, hard.

Introduce jumping. Go through the 1-2-3-4 sequence again. Don't let him head it without jumping. This will encourage him to move forward to meet the ball if it is a lower throw.

Increase the power of the ball coming towards him by kicking it. Same sequence . . .

Now jump to head kicked balls . . . from side to side, as well.

Bring in contact and competition by going through the earlier routines first with another player standing passively close to the header to distract. Then make it an active challenge for each ball by both of them.

1. Heading in pairs for more active practices is universally popular and this is good for control and accuracy. In training the Hungarians used it a great deal, sometimes when they were seated or kneeling. Individually a player does not necessarily have to be able to reach the world record of over 1,000 consecutive headers by a schoolboy, but it is a fine way of exercising the neck muscles and improving control.

2. For heading judged distances: three players, One, Two, Three in a line, one ball. One throws to Two who heads it back to him to enable him, One, to head it over him to Three, who in turn heads it to the middle man, Two, who returns it to Three, who heads it over him back to One, and so on.

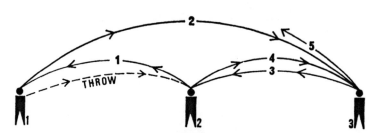

Fig. 4. Heading judged distances.

3. For rapid adjustment pressure on one man: three players in a line, two balls. The man in the middle heads a ball back to the first outside man who has thrown it for him, then turns and does the same to the other man. He is put under pressure by varying the rapidity and difficulty of the balls thrown to him.

4. Adjustment, movement and thought: a player with his back to the thrower or kicker turns on a command from the feeder who throws the ball at the same time for the player to head. Don't give him the same sort of ball twice. Head back and down.

5. Adjustment, movement and conditioning: the same practice as the previous one, but this time the player is lying on the ground when the order is given. This can be an exacting exercise.

6. Throw-Head-Catch game: limited or full-sized. Instead of kicking the ball the player in possession throws the ball to a team mate who must head a pass which can be caught by a colleague or intercepted by the opposition if inaccurate. No running with the ball; no heading to yourself; headed goals only. If it touches the ground either side can retrieve it. Impose restrictions, like 10-yard passes only.

7. For timing and calling: two players, One and Two, head to each other in pairs while a third player circles them at a jog. Watching the two players, Three calls for the ball, by name, and that player must head the ball to where he is in the circle in such a way that he can head it back and the practice continue.

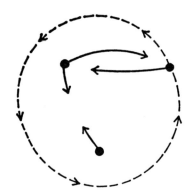

Fig. 5. Timing, calling and heading.

8. Thought, control, movement and calling: a group of players are numbered from One upwards. They must head the ball in numerical sequence, but not in a circle. The only way to do it is for the players to keep an eye on the one who is the number in front of him, get himself in a position where he can receive the ball from him. As he himself heads he should call out the next man's number to make sure he locates him.

9. Head Tennis: this is a wonderfully competitive game for heading and ball control. Limit the players to a certain number

of touches each side of the net. The use of side walls makes the game faster and more advanced.

The extreme to aim for is the skill of Wynn Davies, the best header of a ball in British football. He is the supreme example of courage and confidence in the air. The fact that he has had forty-six stitches in his face and head during his professional career might not recommend the game to the faint-hearted, but it is a testimony of his great courage.

Examples of players who head the ball well are Hateley, Law, Cliff Jones, Charnley, McIlmoyle, Ron Davies, Ritchie, Lord. Defensively Charlie Hurley is probably the best in Britain at the moment. England, Miller and Jack Charlton are three more defenders who stand out in the air. Most of these men are tall and strong, but height is not necessarily a condition of skill in the air. Cliff Jones is only 5 ft. 6½ in. tall; Law is capable of outjumping anyone and he is 5 ft 9 in. And, of course, the West German centre-forward Uwe Seeler, the smallest man in their forward line, has always been a great problem to defences in the air.

CHAPTER TEN

Running with the Ball

There are few better sights in football than players like Charlton, Osgood, Best, Cliff Jones, Morgan or Eusebio running at speed with the ball—control, artistry, fluency, and a dash which means excitement for the spectator and danger for the opposition. In British football it is a rare sight. Foreign players seem generally more composed on the ball, more comfortable in flight. As a skill in Britain, running with the ball is not recognised unless as a sort of dribbling which is either taken for granted as a natural gift or discarded as dangerous and destructive to team play. This is not so. Players who cannot run with the ball, and that is the majority, are forced to kick—or try to run with it, often losing possession. The ability to run with the ball is the foundation of the skill of beating a man. Practices are simple to organise, ideal for warming up, enjoyable—and necessary.

The basic principles: to develop a way of running naturally and to be able to play the ball without hampering the stride or style. This is best achieved by turning the feet inwards, pushing the ball forward with the outside of the foot. The running stride with or without the ball should vary very little. A player should restrict the number of times he touches the ball in a run. Touching it too often will reduce his speed. In practices, try to ensure that the players pick up a moving ball rather than a still one. And running with the ball includes controlling it with the thigh, chest, head as well as the foot.

1. Threes: players One and Two are across the opposite side of the penalty area to Three. One runs to Three, Three to Two, and Two to One and so on; outside of one foot, then the other; alternate outsides; five, four and three touch across the area; stop in the middle and off again; take the ball across in the air.

In runs with restricted number of touches, the habit of playing prevents them from playing it too far ahead.

2. Relay races: the element of competition will make the practices more difficult and interesting.

3. Ins and Outs: inside of one foot, outside of that foot, the inside of the other foot, outside of that foot. This has even professionals struggling at the start. The temptation to use the convenient foot after one or two touches is overpowering. But slowly at first, then in threes and relay races, the players are forced into body movement and balanced runs.

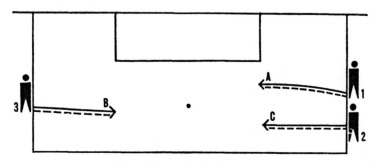

Fig. 6. Running and control.

The value of dribbling around sticks in a line is doubtful. Of course it is better than nothing, but I am not at all enthusiastic about the practice. The good player can go through with either little movement of his body or change of direction. A bad player is here, there and everywhere. In fact, body movement is a development of the art of running with the ball. Instant change of direction at speed makes more impression on a game than beating a man.

In threes and in relays, feint to stop, to turn, to change pace, to go one way and then the other.

Tricks: young players learn tricks willingly and quickly. Older players, sometimes with some sort of trick at their command, resist anything new and when they are forced to try it, are surprisingly incompetent, even at professional level. First, practise one trick at a time in threes and relays.

Examples: *Itchy Cow.* Moving the foot quickly forwards and backwards over the ball like a cow scratching itself. This gives the impression of a stop or back-heel.

E 65

Kick Back. Withdrawing the leg into back swing quickly as if preparing to kick the ball.

Step Over. As the non-kicking foot strikes the ground to the side and slightly in front of the ball, move the other foot inside the ball, around in front of it and back to drag it on as that foot completes a restricted stride.

Stopping or *checking the ball*: a question of balance.

Young and inexperienced players will usually settle for one trick. Once they develop a preference the target should be confidence and perfection in that trick—not competence in a few. After all, players with only one trick get away with it for years.

Going past a player: in the chapter on speed I wrote about the principles of using speed to the utmost by pushing the ball well past the opponent, not a short distance, and then accelerating after it. Remember, every attempted deception, feint, twist, and turn, however simple, should be followed immediately by acceleration. This was Stanley Matthews's great strength. Watch Charlton and Greaves today in particular. A one-pace player with all the tricks in the world is easy to contain because he cannot get away from the man he has deceived.

The highest example of control and deception in British football is George Best. He moves beautifully with the ball. Change of direction is always at his command and he is one of the few players to have several tricks up his sleeve. He has lately developed well one of the fashionable tricks of the moment, playing the ball through an opponent's legs, not so much when he is in front of him, but when he is running alongside.

Players who run particularly well with the ball at speed are Charlton, probably the most controlled, Greaves, Osgood, Thompson, Tambling, Hurst, Stringfellow, Sinclair, Paine, Jones (Cardiff), Brabrook, Summerbee, Johanneson, Clarke (WBA), Rees, Connelly, Harrison, Cliff Jones, Hector, Morgan, Coates and Cooke.

Temple's goal for Everton in the 1966 Cup Final was a fine display of running at speed with the ball, of not playing it too often, of having it under close enough control to be able to put in a perfect shot at the right instant.

Most good professionals develop the art of feints and most have some sort of body swerve. Brabrook in particular has one of the most pronounced body swerves. Crossan can play the ball rapidly from foot to foot four or five times in the space of a yard or two to put the defender off balance. Charlton's feint to kick fools plenty of the best defenders who are well aware of his style and the trick.

CHAPTER ELEVEN

Tackling

I shall never be sure which is the more important, knowing how to tackle or knowing when to tackle. Knowing the latter without the former would be of little help to anyone, so first I shall concentrate on How.

Tackling is the hardest skill to teach. Practice is uncomfortable and more often than not unrealistic. Theory means less here than in any other aspect of the game. I regularly see players who appear to do everything wrong but still come out of a tackle with the ball. This makes them right, and provided a player is winning the ball and not breaking the laws or limbs, I would never change his technique for the sake of theory.

Tackling is 70 per cent determination. In less skilled grades of soccer the element of determination might be even more necessary, for poorer ball control, smaller pitches, and 50/50 balls bring tackling into the game more frequently and make it slightly less a test of judgement and technique. Size has little to do with it, although it helps. Bremner is 5 ft. 6 in. tall and weighs only just 10 stone. Stiles is 5 ft. 5 in. and 10 st. 10 lb. And their tackling lacks nothing. British footballers, however, are no longer tackling for everything. Today everyone, not only defenders, is expected to be able to tackle.

Basic principles: weight—players are quite prepared to get their legs involved in a tackle, but not their bodies. This is the road to injury, bruises, kicks and failure. A player should use his weight to the utmost advantage within the rules of the game. If he does not use his whole body and is a small player he will have a limited value in the side. If he is a big player his size probably contributes to the reason for selecting him in the first place. Most coaching books picture two players in identical positions tackling each other in an identical way for the ball—weight on the tackling foot, head over the ball, shoulder to shoulder, looking down, grim-faced. Basically this is correctness itself, but taken to the point of idealism. The one in possession originally is at fault for allowing himself to get involved in that situation. A player can still tackle correctly without adhering to all those points, but he will not tackle firmly unless he has his weight backing him up.

Sliding should be discouraged. Tackling is not merely a question of depriving the opponent of the ball. It is retaining possession of it. Slide tackling is for desperate circumstances when the ball is to be made dead, over the goal-line or touch-line, or to pass-tackle to another player. As a habit, it encourages slackness, impatience and foolhardy commitment. Players must remain on their feet. When young footballers begin to develop fire in their play, sliding on soft ground appeals to them. As most of them are one-sided the tendency is to tackle with the good foot only.

Don't allow this. Insist that a player remains on his feet. He will be unable to reach a situation he might have reached had he slid at it. By standing up, he will not be able to tackle from as far away. Automatically adjustment is demanded of him. The nearer he gets, the easier it is for him to stand up and tackle. But the nearer he gets the more he must be on his toes. To stand up and tackle he must await the right moment. Without even mentioning the words, jockeying and containing an opponent have been introduced into his play. A good tackle needs patience, determination and the ability to strike like a snake.

Shirkers: fear is a difficult thing to conquer. Lack of confidence is more straightforward. Detailed analysis has revealed that tough training with an over-emphasis on physical contact does little to help a player who is frightened. But he might become more determined if he is told that his skill is up to standard and only his tackling is keeping him from being an automatic selection.

Practices: going through the motions and principles of tackling in pairs helps very little, I have found, and only encourages half-heartedness. But with extremely inexperienced players it is necessary. From there, as much action as possible.

1. One against One: in a confined area with a bucket or something as a goal which minimises long kicking and encourages possession.

2. Two against Two: with a goal again, as above.

3. Nine defenders, including a goalkeeper and two playing out and attacking, alternating frequently.

4. The first two practices are suitable for indoor training, as is this one. Playing on a very hard surface, indoors or outdoors, will often help players grasp the point of remaining on their feet and tackling from a better balanced position. In this practice two teams of players—and the number can vary from two to ten or eleven—are lined up facing each other 30 yards apart. Each team is numbered. The coach calls out a number, say Five, and the two players numbered Five fight for possession of the ball between the two teams, trying to dribble it through the opposition's line of players. When the coach shouts another number the first two leave the ball and return to the line.

Examples of tackling: when Dave Mackay first joined Spurs from Hibernian I saw him play and thought he would never make a First Division player. He was fearless, but late with his tackles, and frequently over-committed himself. After three months he was still breaking all the laws of theory, but he was getting the ball, often and fairly. For some years he has stood out as the best tackler in the game, particularly through the speed of his strike. Yet he remains a difficult man to copy, for he tackles at moments when he is alone, outnumbered, off balance. He takes a lot of knocks and injuries. If he is to be cited as an example of anything, it must be of determination.

Determination made Nobby Stiles a strong tackler and a World Cup player. If he were as quiet and retiring on the field as he is off it I doubt whether he would be playing for a club like Manchester United. I don't think he would be a First Division footballer and certainly not an England regular, despite the fact that he reads the game superbly. But determination is not noise, it is action.

CHAPTER TWELVE

Trapping and Ball Control

If I gathered a group of players round me, held the ball out to one of them, said to him "Eat it", and then threw the ball at his feet, his first reaction would be to trap the ball, or try to, and then think about the wisdom of what I had said.

I believe the surest way of bringing sharpness and naturalness into trapping and ball control—a development of it—is by throwing the game at the players. Or in this case, the ball and the situation.

Watch the ten players of a good professional side trap the ball and control it. Their methods will vary considerably, and each player will have his own preference. Ball control is not so much a question of having a variety of methods of controlling the ball as being able to control in a variety of circumstances.

First the player should be introduced briefly to the methods to prevent naturalness, one foot bias particularly, going unrestrained and becoming a weakness. Then he should be thrown into the middle of action and made to sort it out for himself.

Basic principles of trapping: to trap a ball dead, part of the body and the ground must together form a wedge. The angle of the ground will not vary much, so the angle of the other half of the wedge must change according to where the ball is coming from. Body balance must be considered carefully. It is far easier to keep balanced if the player can trust himself to trap with both feet, instead of relying on one.

Practices:

1. Pushing the ball hard along the ground. Trap it with
   i. The sole of the foot (the most obvious wedge principle).
   ii. The inside of the foot (the most common).

   iii. The outside of the foot (the one to be most encouraged
      because it is the most useful).
   iv. The shin.
  2. Introduce movement, sideways and forwards.
  3. Throw the ball in the air. Then use the same four methods,
first standing still, then with movement, sideways and forwards.

A footballer can very seldom afford to trap a ball dead and
remain motionless in a game. If he can, he has done well to put
himself in such a clear position.

Trap control: a development of the first stage, this is the skill
of getting out of trouble and into a better position, or making
immediate progress by retaining possession of the ball by trapping and playing it away in one movement.

Use the outside of the foot as much as possible and play the
ball the way you are facing, first from a standing position, then
moving sideways and forwards. If there are enough players
sufficiently advanced, put a passive defender behind the player
receiving the ball. From there bring in feinting and body
movement before the moment of contact. Then make the
defender active.

Chest trapping and control: to kill the ball, bring the shoulders forward, forming a concave chest. To trap control the ball
on the chest, push the chest out a little to give the ball controlled
rebound off the body, turning in the direction the ball should go.

Small games: inexperienced players, in the excitement and
stress of a game, will kick, dribble or pass, but they will rarely
control a ball. The coach must force them to do this. Five- or
six-a-sides will bring all the players into the game. Conditions—
two touch, three touch if they are young, no tackling if they are
unskilled—will put stress on their control. But the rhythm of the
game must be Control, Play, Control, Play. The coach should
not allow them to play in too much of a hurry. Initially they will
lose something in their game. Eventually the benefit will make
the routine worthwhile.

Ball control: when Puskas was playing for Hungary against
Scotland he made the crowd gasp when he caught a goal kick
from Grosics on his foot, turned and dropped it down to the
ground and made off with it. He had developed to the extreme
the timing and sensitivity of his feet and the art of cushioning.

A ball driven against a wall will rebound. A ball driven against a cushion will flop lifelessly. Taking the pace out of the ball and controlling it involves using the body as a cushion by giving in to the ball—but not too much. It is all a question of sensitivity, which is another word for practice.

Juggling: Puskas himself began a trend in 1953 which has grown out of all proportion since. As he waited for the kick-off at Wembley, against England, he passed the time with some ball juggling which caught the crowd's eye—foot, thigh, head, shoulders. He rolled it down his back, back-heeled and was off again. To some, the Hungarian victory was as much a triumph for ball juggling as for their other skills. Ball juggling seemed to sweep the land. But somewhere along the line it lost its point. Mastery of the ball comes highest on the list of priority skills—but mastery in match situations. Professionals develop a wealth of individual tricks—Dave Mackay puts on a great show with billiard balls, Rodney Marsh with an orange, and so on—because of the hours they spend in the company of a ball or of footballers. Amateurs and young players tend to copy these incidental skills before they have a grounding in the more basic realistic skills.

A twelve-year-old Swedish boy who recently spent part of his holiday at Maine Road could keep the ball up for as many as 900 touches. David Burnside, as a youngster, was equally exceptional and even put on half-time performances for the crowd —all the fruits of hard work with a tennis ball, in Burnside's case usually on a railway station. But it worries me that they should have spent so long perfecting a skill which is hardly part of football when they were practising with the idea of improving their game. Time is so short, and if ball juggling is to be introduced into practice, for groups or individuals, then it must be made as realistic as possible.

Three touches: each player passing it on to another player with the third touch, or if a player is alone, hitting the ball against a wall and catching the rebound. Use the weak foot only. Or groups of three touches on each foot, thigh, head. Use movement, up and down the pitch or the garden, keeping the ball up.

Puskas and Kocsis had their own two touch practice. Standing 20 or 30 yards apart, one would volley the ball to the other to control with one touch and volley it back. They did not lob it, but hit it hard, sometimes as many as twenty times before the ball touched the ground. Di Stefano would often carry the ball 20 yards in the air, on his head or thigh, in a match.

Mastery, yes. Ball juggling, yes. But don't forget the game of football or it will pass you by.

The nearer the ground, the easier the ball is to control. Players have not the time to wait for the ball and control it in its easiest position. The skill of ball control hinges on how a player copes with a ball in the air. This is where players should be forced into the middle of things. Control and play, once again. Make it life-like, and difficult, by meeting the ball.

1. Teams of eight players are 40 to 50 yards away from the coach or another player who has the ball which is kicked towards them in the air. The player sprints towards the ball, controls it as early as possible in its flight, and plays it back to the server. A kick of 25 to 30 yards is ideal with the ball arriving at various heights and speeds.

2. Now smash the ball at the players, accurately. They should not be allowed to wait and receive the ball. Not only must they meet the ball, judging its flight and speed, they have also to contend with the difficulties of wind, ground and movement.

3. As the player arrives on the ball the coach shouts either "Attack" or "Defend", and the player either controls and plays the way he is facing or turns and feeds it back.

4. Now "Left", "Right", "Attack", "Defend"—and always sprinting to meet the ball.

5. A player is under pressure, individually, in a circle of players. They feed him with throws to control and play to a specified point; or behind a line which he leaves to meet the ball and control, but must regain before the next throw.

6. Small games: two touch, 15-yard passes only.

7. Control and kicking in positional situations. Firm, long balls are hit to players in their positions on the field to control and turn . . . wing-half to centre-forward who meets the ball, controls and turns; goalkeeper to wingers, etc. Put a defender, first passive then active, on to the man controlling the ball.

8. Taking the pace off the ball, trapping, cushioning, turning, can be practised alone by kicking any sort of ball against a wall.

Turning: this is the most specialised art in the game, calling for courage as well as skill. The masters were Jimmy Logie, Wilf Mannion, Di Stefano and Sivori.

"Play it the way you are facing," is a familiar cry from coaches. The Russians rarely do anything else and their play often lacks imagination and inspiration as a result. At a high level, football without the sort of player who dares turn with the ball becomes predictable, at a low level, ordinary. Certain players cannot do it, others should not do it, and defenders should try not to allow it. That is why it is so valuable . . . and why the Italians are prepared to pay so much for a good inside-forward, one who, despite the tight marking, fierce tackling, defensive covering, can still turn with the ball, under pressure, and pass accurately.

Many of the practices already mentioned involve turning, or can be adapted to do so, but for mid-field players try this.

From a distance of 20 to 30 yards hit a ball at the player who must meet the ball, control and turn. At the instant when he first touches the ball a defender can move in on him from the same starting-point. Gradually reduce the turner's advantage by making him start from behind the defender, until they are both challenging for the ball together. If it seems difficult, remember there are few players in professional football who can turn with the ball under pressure.

Examples in professional football: Pele, Sivori, Suarez, Law, Greaves, Charlton, Best, Baker, Young, St. John, Byrne, Osgood, Baxter, Puskas, Eusebio. South Americans are often considerably more able than Europeans in ball control, partly because of the emphasis on virtuosity and the condition of their grounds, as well as questions of temperament. In the World Cup Pele found that even his control was not good enough to get out of trouble against tight and ruthless marking. But he suffered mainly through playing in a bad side which gave him little assistance.

CHAPTER THIRTEEN

Goalkeeping

All goalkeepers are not as mad as the stories about them would have us believe. If they do seem strange at times it is hardly surprising, considering how they are treated in practice and training.

A goalkeeper is not a footballer. He is the odd man out in any team. In most clubs he is regarded as some sort of outcast. He makes up the numbers. He is there to be shot at whenever anyone feels like it. If he makes a mistake in a match he is, as everyone quietly suspected from the start, useless.

Goalkeepers go between the posts for one of two reasons usually . . . either they have a natural aptitude for it or they are no good outside. This is not as cruel as it sounds. Peter Shilton went into goal in the first place because all the other positions in his class team were occupied. That was at the age of seven. At sixteen he played in a First Division match. At seventeen he is Gordon Banks's deputy at Leicester with a number of England Youth caps to his credit. But for whatever reason the goalkeeper puts on the jersey he must have help from others. He must have concentrated practice designed for him alone. He must spend a lot of time working in the area in which he competes . . . the goal.

He is the most important individual on the field. If he is playing well he raises the game of the players in front of him. If he plays badly the team will probably lose regardless of how other players perform. Hungary failed to reach the World Cup semi-final for one reason only—they could not produce a goalkeeper of international standard. A number of other World Cup teams suffered from a similar failure.

One or two of these goalkeepers, men of considerable experience and skill, looked like outfield players suddenly thrown into the job. They seemed incapable of catching the ball. A goalkeeper is a handball player. Handling, catching, gathering that ball, is his privilege. Dropping it is an abuse of that privilege. It's a sin. The ball must become part of him as it is part of a basketball player. He must look upon the safe catching of a ball as a wicket-keeper does, but for the goalkeeper it is more difficult because he must use both hands.

A goalkeeper does not need to be included in every team training activity. Long runs help him very little except at the beginning of the season. An hour of exercises would be far more beneficial. Before anything starts, the coach should ask himself one question. Is this specifically helping the goalkeeper? If it is not, then make him practise his own skills alone, using rebounds off a wall, with another player or goalkeeper or anyone who happens to be available. Handling and catching are the top priorities.

He should handle the ball so frequently he develops the feeling of strength in his fingers, hands and wrists. But he needs more strength than that. Players do not realise how fast and hard a shot travels at a goalkeeper, though not everyone in goal will be confronted with David Herd of Manchester United, whose shots in practice have recorded 72 m.p.h. To protect their goal from the fiercest shots goalkeepers cannot afford to dispense with pure strength to resist the force of the shots and the use of their body as a second line of defence. Watch a good goalkeeper make an emergency ground save. If he cannot catch it, he *hits* the ball away—it does not hit him. To dive and put up a barrier against a powerfully hit shot at full strength calls for strong arms and shoulders. Grosics, the great Hungarian goalkeeper, worked hard with a heavy medicine ball, and Jack Kelsey was one of many who used weights.

The goalkeeper should be the best kicker of the ball in the team. He is usually the worst, because he gets least practice. He is expected to be able to kick a still ball, as well as one out of his hands, accurately over the halfway line or make a short pass precisely to a defender. This is asking a great deal. To bring a goalkeeper more into the game, play him out of goal in practice occasionally, allowing him to catch the ball, put it down and kick it or throw it. Make certain he is involved in the practices for accurate kicking.

Match practice and training practice for goalkeepers are as different as shadow boxing and a fight. Conventional shooting in and crosses will help his handling, catching and judgement. To cope with the unexpected, the mis-hits, the unsighted shots, the rebounds, the changes of direction which a match will throw upon him, a goalkeeper needs agility, spring, and physical and mental speed to cover the huge area of the goal. Diving must become an instinct to him. To help this, handicap him in these practices:

1. He lies down on the goal-line with his head near a post. From the edge of the area, shots are hit into the goal. A fraction before the ball is kicked shout "Up"—and the goalkeeper must spring up and try to save the shot. It is a tough practice. The severity is varied by the power of the shot, the area of the goal it is aimed for and the timing of the order or the position of the goalkeeper—he can have his feet by the post.

2. He stands on the line with his back to the field. At "Go", given as the ball is kicked, he must turn and position himself for shots aimed from various points outside the area.

3. The goalkeeper kneels on the goal-line and from a short distance shots are half-hit at him. The object is to make him stretch for balls and catch them to improve his handling, reactions and suppleness of the top half of his body.

Grosics included high jumping and gymnastics in his training to improve his spring and suppleness. Bert Williams, the Wolves and England goalkeeper, walked seven miles to the ground every day on his toes with the same object. He had incredibly developed calf-muscles.

A knowledge of angles is largely a mark of experience and instinct. That knowledge can be speeded up provided the basic geometry of the problem of narrowing angles is understood. Put a small stick eight yards out and directly between the posts. This will make a triangle of three goals. By making a young goalkeeper defend all three goals he will be encouraged to think in terms of basic angles. The surest way is through familiarity with the goal. Watch most professional goalkeepers. They touch a post to check their position. They do not need to look for the post. Many make a mark about six yards out in line with the penalty spot which, by a quick glance, will give them their position.

The goalkeeper is in charge of the penalty area, but he cannot be expected to be responsible for every square yard of it. Over-emphasis of the penalty area role encourages some goalkeepers to wander about, giving advice like a spectator caught in the middle of things.

A goalkeeper's obsession should be the protection of the goal. It is his property, his responsibility, and one which should never be left open.

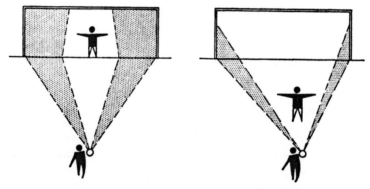

Fig. 7. The basic geometry of narrowing the angle.

If he leaves the goal to narrow the angle it is to hide the goal from the oncoming forwards. If he leaves the goal to exploit the advantage of hands and height, it is to get rid of the danger to his goal, either by confiscating the ball or by punching it well out of harm's way. It is not his job to get mixed up with a situation where his chances of getting the ball are the same as or only a little better than the other players.

Conversely, he should be restricted as little as possible. If he feels it is natural to run out and catch the ball on the far side of the penalty area, then let him do so. Naturalness is only correct if it succeeds.

He must be certain of either getting the ball during the situation, if he cannot get it beforehand, or he must stay close to his main responsibility and see how the situation develops.

Crosses are a goalkeeper's biggest everyday problem. As

the ball comes over he must look for two things—the earliest point in the air where he can get it and nobody else can, and the path on the ground which will allow him to get to the flight of the ball.

He should naturally be strong on crosses because of his advantage. But if that advantage is cancelled out by distance or too many players he should wait and keep the goal intact. Watch how Bonetti, Sprake, Banks and Springett deal with crosses.

Many goalkeepers abandon the role of protector when they are forced to come out of the goal to meet a forward. By diving at his feet too early the majority of the goal is left open. Their best chance of blocking a shot or keeping the goal protected as well as possible for as long as possible in an extreme situation is by standing up. This is a vital principle. The chances of making a save by a reflex action or blocking the ball are greatly increased by standing up. A dive is irrevocable commitment.

The number of goals I have heard blamed on goalkeepers by managers because "he lost his concentration" is legion. But remember, this is the most uncomfortable position of any outdoor game. He suffers the worst of the weather conditions. If water has collected anywhere on the pitch it will be where he has to dive. He is out of the game for long spells. He is limited in what he can do to keep warm.

Nevertheless, he must be forced to concentrate, first by following every action of the game, then by directing his entire attention at the ball when it is in his vicinity. Keeping warm will mean that in ninety minutes he will take almost as much exercise as the outfield players. He cannot expect to perform any feat of agility with a cold body.

In training it is a help to play five-a-side in front of the goalkeeper across the pitch while he is having handling practice. With crosses and shots make a forward or two run in at him as he gathers the ball. Goalkeeping is a lonely job. At times it must be made lonelier by dismissing every possible distraction.

Nervousness or lack of confidence in a goalkeeper points to one result—goals. His faults will affect the performance of the players in front of him. Few clubs pay enough attention to the fact that a confident goalkeeper will raise the game of the ten other players and dishearten the opposition. But no forward perks up quicker than when he sees a goalkeeper fumble his shot or centre.

All the critics pointed to the comparatively poor showing of goalkeepers in the World Cup. Nobody pinpointed why this was so. I'm sure it had a lot to do with confidence. Tension affects a goalkeeper more than other players or, at least, it is more noticeable. The only Europeans who remained unscathed were Banks, who was at home, and Yashin, who has vast experience. Of the others, only the Uruguayan, Mazurkieviez, looked consistently World Cup class. But it is inconceivable that countries like Hungary, Portugal, Brazil and even Germany could not produce an above average goalkeeper. Many of these so-called failures are still in their international teams and probably deservedly so.

There seemed to be something wrong with their psychological preparation. Carvalho, the first Portuguese goalkeeper, did not relish Eusebio using him for shooting practice at their Cheshire training ground, and made it quite obvious. Eusebio could easily have destroyed his confidence with his heart-breaking shots. Carvalho lasted only one match.

If I were lucky enough to have Eusebio in my team I would not allow him to shoot at a recognised goalkeeper in earnest from less than 30 yards in training. In the same way more normal forwards should not be allowed to have practice shots at the goalkeeper from 10 yards. This will not help the goalkeeper. It encourages him to be half-hearted. Make it lifelike and useful or put a makeshift goalkeeper between the posts.

These are some of the general principles. For some of the finer points I have taken Bert Williams as an example and an aid. Not only was he one of England's best goalkeepers, but he has the gift of being able to instruct others. Here are a few of his opinions on goalkeepers' problems.

From one goalkeeper to another. Bert Williams talking.

Practice: everyone thinks you are there to pick their wonderful shots out of the net. You are not. Either they are sensible about it and give you some real practice, or go off and do some training on your own. I hated practice games, with players displaying skills they would never have the confidence to perform in matches. Bear this out and remember—the forward who might beat you with a chip in practice will probably try to break

F

81

the net in a game. So practise what you have been taught. Stand up. You will frighten the life out of him and save it.

Crosses: be natural, but be definite. If you dither, the defence will dither.

Catching: finger tips must make first contact with the ball, taking some of the sting and speed. If the ball hits the palms first there is a greater likelihood of it bouncing out, particularly the modern ball with a plastic strengthened cover. Keep the forearms parallel as much as possible. It will make catching surer and offer another safety barrier. It is a mortal sin to knock the ball down. Never, never do it. Catch it always.

Ground Shots: gather ground shots bending at the waist, keeping the legs straight. Do not go down on one knee. If the ball bounces awkwardly or changes direction suddenly you are rooted to the spot on one knee. The standing position also ensures that the hands are turned palms upwards. The ball will roll naturally on to the hands, up the arms, on to the chest.

Punching: catching is much better unless you are forced to reach for the ball over, rather than at the side of, a bunch of players. Use two hands if the ball is to be punched roughly in the direction it came from, one hand if it is a cross to be diverted.

Safety: I was often accused of being spectacular because I dived for balls as close as a yard from me. I did this to make sure I had my body behind the ball when I caught it. You have to get off your feet to do this. Don't worry about what people say. Safety is much more important than criticism.

Fitness: this is a question of determination and dedication. A goalkeeper must be strong and supple to be agile. Lateral, abdominal and stretching exercise should feature predominantly in his training. Stand on a doorstep or the stairs, or terracing, and exercise until you can touch the next step down. From the press-up position walk your hands into your legs without bending your knees. Walk on the tips of your toes as far as you can to develop spring in your legs.

There are a thousand and one things you can do every spare minute to increase suppleness and strength.

Speed: you need as much speed as any other player, if not more. Do not excuse yourself from sprints because you might not like them.

Moving Out: I liked to encourage the forward to shoot where

I wanted him to. My line of movement out of the goal was aimed slightly to the side of the oncoming forward, giving him an uneven view of the goal. As he shaped to shoot into the larger portion I was ready to try and smother the ball. Once you decide to move out, get on with it. Never back-pedal. This is a sign of fear and doubt about your decision. If you have made a mistake, keep going. It will keep you on your toes.

Projection: in their early days Fred Davies, the Wolves goalkeeper, and Gilbert Merrick, the Birmingham and England goalkeeper, were restricted to reaching shots within their own body length when they dived. This is not enough for a goalkeeper. He must be able to project himself beyond this limitation by agility and strength in his legs. Remain on your toes all the time. It takes longer than you think to move off your heels on to your toes.

Strength: forwards are violent in front of goal. You must be physically capable of standing up to anything they kick at you.

Aggression: outfield players seem to think it makes life much easier if you are allowed to catch the ball. It often makes it much tougher. If you want the ball you must tell them so. If you go for it, do not be frightened of scattering everyone to get it. They will blame you if you fail to make it yours. Forwards often panic when they are confronted with an aggressive goalkeeper.

A Pull-Back (an opponent reaching the goal line with the ball): you are in serious trouble. Do not make it worse by playing yourself out of the game. Normally it will be best to stay on the near post and make him pull the ball back. A bad centre might come to you. A good one will be followed by a shot and you are still in the goal with a slight chance. If you leave the near post you might get the centre. But he might decide not to centre. You are out of the game if you fail to grab it and the last chance of protection is completely sacrificed. Others will be falling back. They might cut out the centre. They have less chance of cutting out the shot.

Positioning for a Cross: it is easier to go forward than backwards. Stand nearer the back of the goal for a cross. If the opponent moves infield with the ball come forward to meet him either to narrow the angle or go to the near post.

Dominate: a goalkeeper can see better than anyone else on the

83

field. Defenders cannot always see you but they can always hear you. It is not your privilege to control the penalty area, it is your job.

Penalties: Yashin says he decides which way he is going to dive by the way the kicker runs up to the ball. He then dives and hopes for the best. Unless you are going to cheat this is quite sound advice. A correctly taken penalty kick takes 0.05 sec. to travel the distance. This takes some stopping, even for goalkeepers.

PART 3: THE TEAM PLAYER

CHAPTER FOURTEEN

The Compact Unit

Take a close look at most schoolboy teams. As the forwards are fighting it out in the opponents's half, or even in the process of shooting, the full-backs, out of habit, will often be positioned at the other end of the pitch, just outside the penalty area. The team will be stretched almost the length of the pitch. This is not exclusively a habit of junior football, but even there, and at other levels where the examples are less extreme—it should be discouraged.

Footballers make up a team, but to legislate categorically that the team unit should be as compact as possible conjures up visions of footballers rushing around in packs after the ball. Even those schoolboys have graduated beyond that. Compactness is influenced by basic positional sense, depth and width, and things like the size of the pitch and how the game is going.

Compactness cannot be a rigid rule. Individual attacks which break down drag players into all parts of the field. But it is safe to generalise that a team should move *en bloc*, like a basketball squad, up and down the pitch, and if necessary from side to side if the pitch is wide enough to allow it.

Too much space between players courts danger, saps the strength of numbers and offers space to the opposition. Compactness in the shape of backing up by the defence and the withdrawal of forwards when the ball is at extreme ends of the pitch are obvious examples. But it is not the fact of the full-backs pushing up to within about 10 yards of the half-way line or forwards coming back to the same distance from the half-way line which achieves the sort of compactness that I am aiming for.

This is part of it. The real test is the speed with which it is achieved—and midfield. Good teams retain this compactness when the ball is in midfield. Where are the forwards when the opposition have worked the ball from their penalty area into midfield? Are they back or just coming back? A team that has won possession in their own penalty area and then lost the ball 30 or 40 yards up the pitch is at its most vulnerable—unless the defence has closed up fast around the ball.

This has nothing to do with the offside law. I have never played to exploit that law. It is dangerous for the team and unhealthy for the players. The amount of movement is governed by the position of the ball, not the opposition.

All the best club teams in the world have compactness: Penerol, Real Madrid, Inter, Liverpool, Chelsea, West Ham, Manchester United. It was the most obvious feature of England's World Cup team display. Many people confuse compactness with defensive football. Because they see ten players defending, they are blinded to the fact that the same team have ten attacking. Attackers need space, so the compactness of the ten in attack must be less concentrated than in defence. It becomes defensive football when the players are restricted in their attacking roles.

One of the biggest fallacies in football suggests that Manchester United are an attacking team. They never have been, or at least not for the last ten years. United rarely have more than two or three forwards up. They depend on the compactness of the team at the back to transform defence into attack.

The best example of a team destroyed by allowing itself to be stretched was Benfica playing against Manchester United in the 1966 quarter-final of the European Cup. Germano rarely came out of his penalty area, and in the second leg the Portuguese forwards' urgency for goals left the midfield to United. They won 5–1 in Lisbon, 8–3 on aggregate.

Compactness is not just a theory. To put it into practice the running of individual players must be improved—distance and speed. It increases a player's involvement and work in the game without reducing his individual responsibilities. Players work far harder in the game now than when I was playing. Captains a few years ago seemed to spend all their time trying to persuade forwards, wingers particularly, to run, run, run, instead of waiting to be served. Every team needs at least one driving personality, but preferably two or three players, at the back who can exhort the others and keep them together. Talking is good when it is constructive.

Vocal drive and fitness will achieve only partial results. Without aggression the team will lack that vital spark which is the difference between regaining the ball and merely preventing the other side playing; the difference between standing one yard off an opponent with the ball and standing five yards from him; the difference between getting a hard shot in and aiming at the goal.

People talk about cowards in professional sport. I doubt if there are any. Certainly some play more aggressively than others. Some players, at any level, cannot take knocks consistently week after week. Incredibly, broken legs to some like Mackay (twice) and Lord (three times) seem to make no difference to their spirit. I doubt if it will affect Peter Osgood much. He is still likely to become one of the greatest players of this age. Whatever a player's temperament or character, his determination and aggression can be increased—unless he is a Hurst, a Stiles or a Mackay, who already have it in full. And this is the job of the coach. From the very beginning he is backed by the most powerful weapon anyone in charge of others could wish for—the weapon of being right. No player can deny the need for aggression. They have only to look at themselves in action when they are on top.

Good team play is a mental and physical discipline in a match, established largely in training. Training should be hard, the demand on players more than they expect, then more and more. It is natural for players as a group to make do with a minimum of hard work and to expend their energy doing what they like best. This is wrong. They should be made to work hard at everything. Insist, for instance, that they should go for balls in the air if this happens to be a weakness. Put them through 100 repetitions. It sounds like lines to a schoolboy—except for two differences: improvement and enjoyment.

The response to aggressive coaching I have found is the same —aggressive play and enjoyment. Schoolboys, amateurs, university students, professionals, all of them. Whether a player is collecting £160 or contributing 2s. 6d. to the laundry fund, the reason he began playing in the first place is the same—enjoyment. They might grumble at hard training. But a weak coach

87

and half-hearted training they will despise. Discipline and aggression were never the creations of half-heartedness.

Practices:

1. *Man-for-Man marking*: this can be played from five-a-side to full-scale games. It encourages tight marking and discipline, but remember the players' team positional play is sacrificed in favour of his individual job.

2. *The Numbers game*: the players are forced to pass in sequence of numbers. This teaches compactness and necessity of looking for and helping others.

3. *Three against three*: all three must work. This teaches aggression. The slacker stands out. Five against Seven, or any uneven small game, demands more work from the outnumbered.

4. *Shadow Football* (an invention of Alan Brown): the whole team play against only a goalkeeper or two or three defenders. This is a fine way of impressing all levels of positional play on players.

5. *Ghost Football* (*a favourite of Bill Nicholson's*): two teams play shadow football on the same pitch, "through" each other. This encourages compact team play and offers unwitting obstacles.

CHAPTER FIFTEEN

System

As I took my seat on the trainer's bench I hoped what I had told the centre-forward had sunk in. I had certainly told him often enough before, and we had worked on it in practice. It was while I was coaching Sutton United, a useful amateur side, and this particular game counted heavily in their league championship. The centre-forward was a natural left-footer and had the habit of moving out to the wing in front of the left winger. Time and time again he did it. I had tried to cure him, because the left winger was fast and quite capable of beating the full-back, but liked a run at the ball. By continually moving out to the wing the centre-forward reduced the outside-left's space and minimised his penetration.

I was furious when, straight from the kick-off, the centre-forward raced out to the left wing. The ball went to the outside-left, who saw he could not make a run, so pushed it through to the centre-forward. I was still saying some unkind things about him as he took it forward about 15 yards, centred and somebody put it in the back of the net.

So much for system, I expect one or two people thought. So much for Allison, I expect the centre-forward thought. It was just another reminder that circumstances in this game have an embarrassing habit of turning either way, despite plans and system. Rigid adherence to theory sometimes produces results, sometimes stalemate.

I could put a brave face on things in this instance, despite the embarrassment, because we had scored and I knew I was still right. Over a period of time the outside-left, given space and a run, would create more danger than the centre-forward in the same position. You must play the best average in this game, but not exclusively. It will not succeed at each attempt. I suppose the centre-forward could say I was restricting his play. But if it increased the odds of success it was justified. Eventually I cured him of the habit—to the advantage of the team in general, I knew, and to the left winger in particular.

System will not win games. When a team adopts a new system and wins a few matches the credit is often attributed to the system. But it is always players who win or lose matches. Some systems demand more practice than others because they appear more revolutionary and intricate. A change of system varies and shuffles the work rate of players. But the basic principles remain the same, although some might be given more emphasis than others. I do not like talking to players of catenaccio, verrou, the whirl, the bolt, 4-2-4, 4-3-3 and so on. I prefer to give them roles to perform and ensure that they know what the other members of the team are expected to do.

For this is the value of system—it gives players purpose. It encourages them to think together, as a team. Chosen correctly it assists them to exploit their strengths and cover up their weaknesses.

To think in unison players need to talk to each other about the game and the way they are going to play. Tactics are not just one man and a blackboard. Even if enjoyment comes higher on the list of priorities than results, basic discussion always helps to realise a higher potential of skill and satisfaction. It is a mistake to assume that amateurs play the game for enjoyment and professionals play for money. Almost everyone plays to win and improve. Often it is the coach or organiser who finds himself in the job through duty or enjoyment. If he neglects the most obvious method of getting a better team performance and individual improvement—through system and tactics—he is doing the game and the players a great disservice.

It is wrong to think of the latest fashionable systems as primarily restrictive. They can be interpreted that way, but the original idea was usually to cover up weaknesses and bring players into the game more. There is nothing more restrictive than the WM formation and the pivot defence system. The centre-forward and wingers stand watching the game for long spells; the full-backs put their defence in jeopardy if they venture too far upfield; the centre-half and wing-halves are restricted to certain areas of the pitch.

The object, particularly with younger players, should be to give them roles which will restrict them as little as possible. Of course, not everyone will be able to do just what he wants. The role of the centre-half, for instance, has changed very little. He remains a restricted player and he must always have cover. So at the outset there are a minimum of two restricted players.

The factors deciding which system will suit a team best are: the players available, not only their ability but the amount of running and work they are capable of doing; and the standard of the opposition. This is the more important. A team in command of a game does not have a defensive way of playing. There are no bad positions when your side scores a goal, although there might have been a few seconds before the ball went in. The Al Read character who scoffs at a particular player and dramatically changes his tune to "He's a good 'un" when he scores a lucky goal from 40 yards is not so uncommon. Directors' boxes are full of them.

If a team were losing 7–0 week after week, the goalkeeper was not throwing them in, and the wingers were complaining of never getting a touch, I should be inclined to think there was something wrong with the system, whatever the standard of the players.

Years ago football was all hobnails and forwards—nine of them, supported by one full-back and a goalkeeper. The pendulum has swung back too far, for in Italian football and European competition matches as many as seven or eight players are withdrawn into exclusively defensive roles. In professional football there is always a great deal at stake. The rewards of success are just as important as the penalties of failure. Fear of making mistakes, keeping up with the Jones's and rank bad managership, of which there is plenty, will dictate the pattern and character of a game.

Somewhere along the swing of that pendulum, between the two extremes, there lies a more balanced system which is adaptable for all levels of skill. Certainly the need to play defensive football in games below professional grade is less. So is its advisability. As the standard deteriorates, the propor-

91

tion of errors in a game increases. Attacking football produces better results because of the increased opportunities that error and imperfect skills offer. Home and away advantages are less unless there is a large crowd. Observation of the elementary principles of defensive covering will keep a team out of trouble for much of the time. Naturalness and aggression will often gain the upper hand—and there is nothing more natural in football than wanting to score a goal.

Before damning professional teams' defensive policies, examine their strengths and weakness. Do not be deceived by names. There are no more or no less great players than there were twenty or forty years ago. Plenty of teams have none of them in their line-ups, however.

Modern football demands more running and more sharing of the exciting and less exciting aspects of the game. From this point I want to go into the principles of the sort of system which I feel will achieve the best results for any level of football as far as it is possible to generalise, cover the basic necessities and allow players as much freedom as possible. Extra running is a prerequisite. Without it we shall be back at square one very quickly.

CHAPTER SIXTEEN

System and the Players

The ideal, I heard one manager say, is to have a squad of twenty first-team players. Football is not a question of ideals. No team ever has what it wants. But what, within the bounds of realism, does it need? And how does one pick out the qualities of the players available?

In any team I coached, from park to professional level, I would try to find by selection or moulding the following basic needs: a goalkeeper; two full-backs capable of tight marking; a centre-half; midfield men and especially a creative midfield player; a front man; and a striker.

The goalkeeper, the most important specialist, we have talked about earlier. **The centre-half** needs to be disciplined, strong, and the bigger the better provided size does not mean the exclusion of mobility. The qualifications to play in that position seem quite well known. The role of the **full-back** is also not a complicated one. The biggest error many selectors make is forgetting the necessity of speed at the front for attack, which is obvious, and speed at the back for rescue. It is a mistake to put all the speed at the front and the slowest at the back. Remember, a number of professional full-backs began their careers as forwards.

There is little to be said about **strikers.** They are worth their weight in gold, and players capable of scoring goals can be forgiven almost anything except laziness around the penalty area. A striker can be excused specific defensive chores but he must work hard, in practice and in matches, at his own craft. He will still have many yards to run to maintain compactness. The object should be to make everyone one work. A skilled player should not be permitted to depend on his skill alone. Most of them will try to.

Wingers playing in the old-fashioned style are luxuries in anything but an overwhelmingly strong side or with anyone but an overwhelmingly good player. Many footballers are uncomfortable on the touchline and cannot receive a ball there without being forced backwards or inside. If there are players available with the speed, ball control and instinct for touchline play, so much the better. Many wingers are merely less skilled, smaller, slower or younger inside-forwards. It is often a sound policy to pull them back and allow them to play on the touchline from a deeper position.

In the Ipswich championship winning side Leadbetter, originally an inside-forward but by then slower and to some, past his best, was immensely effective lying deep, picking up clearances and linking with the midfield players.

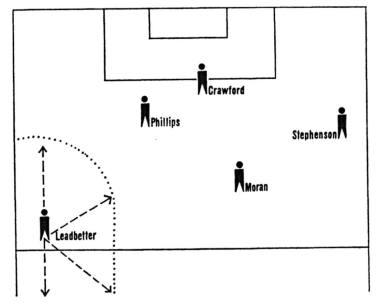

Fig. 8. The Ipswich forward line.

Pulling a winger back creates space in front of him for the forward players. A mobile centre-forward will enjoy this extra room, but passes on the blind side of him—that is, on the outside of him as he moves towards the corner flag—are difficult to control. England used this idea with players like Hunt and Hurst covering great distances.

However wingers are asked to play it is essential that the majority of them should forget the limited roles of the last decade. They must be workers, fetch-and-carry footballers, not stand-and-deliver players like the old days. Watch how Thompson and Callaghan incorporate penetration with the much less spectacular job of helping defenders.

The functions I want to look at in more detail are those of the midfield player with a creative bent and the front man—the first indisputably the hub of a team, the second undiscovered by many teams.

The midfield man: He should be a player who receives the ball easily, which is not as normal as it sounds. Even professional teams produce only three or four with this quality. He needs to be able to turn with the ball, take up positions which make other players look good, see situations quickly and kick well.

His work rate must be very high, but it is not essential for him to be one of the fastest players on the field. In fact, most midfield players usually lack something in speed, for they are milers as opposed to sprinters.

He is not a rigid positional player and the area he covers is limited only by his stamina, although this category of player is often out of place, tactically and temperamentally, in the emergency areas of the field.

A midfield player needs a built-in safety valve, imagination with a touch of conservatism. He must not be caught in possession. As the player who feeds and sparks off those around him he must be prepared to play safe balls which initiate nothing, rather than hope for the best in impossible situations. He does not win games alone, but without him the team performance fluctuates alarmingly.

Defensively he is called on to do more work today than three or four years ago. Then, somebody was detailed to cover up to allow him more freedom. This was the essence of the Danny Blanchflower–Dave Mackay combination and the Pat Crerand–Nobby Stiles link. In some 4-2-4 combinations there are basically six defenders, two of whom put themselves into offensive positions when they can. The best players (Gibson,

Harvey, Ball, Baxter, Boyce, Hunter, Bremner, Harris) can do both roles with limitations.

The midfield man can always do certain negative jobs, like marking at throw-ins and restarts, but once again his tasks will vary according to the opposition. John Crossan (or Colin Bell) of Manchester City must get back to the halfway line as soon as the movement breaks down. If he is still the defensive side of the ball he tries to get into the situation and help close it up unless he can regain the ball immediately, which is rare. He is not allotted an individual man to mark unless an opposing wing-half is destroying us.

The job is hardest when the game is going against his side. Once he stops running and waits for the ball to reach him he becomes just another player. In a young footballer, creation shows itself clearly. The coach's function is often to increase his work rate when things are going badly and prevent him from overdoing things when the game is going well.

Here are some past and present creative midfield players: Wilf Mannion, Peter Doherty, Hideguti, Jimmy Logie, Alex James, John White, Bobby Charlton, Terry Venables, Bobby Collins, Colin Harvey, Alan Ball, George Eastham, Gordon Harris, Gordon Milne, Ron Boyce—called "Clockwork" because, allegedly, he is would up before a game and keeps running for ninety minutes. Di Stefano showed his great ability by being able to work in midfield and defence as well as score goals. Alex James was unequalled at picking up balls in the centre of the field and hitting long, accurate passes almost anywhere.

These men are not often tightly marked if their function goes beyond the conventional inside-forward role. I feel this is wrong. Goal scorers with a flair for doing the right thing are immensely difficult to subdue. Sometimes the task is made less difficult by stifling the source of their service.

The difference between a coach having what he wants and making do will hang largely on the midfield talent he has at his disposal. One midfield player is not enough. The two wing-halves and two inside-forwards are midfield players. But to find four footballers with the qualities I have mentioned smacks of idealism again—and lack of balance.

Wing-halves must obviously be more defensively minded

with clearcut responsibilities and less freedom. Fluidity, however, is the heart of good attacking football and in a good team these players will interchange, cover and run for each other. Manchester United are extremely adaptable in midfield. A wing-half and an inside-forward are often the same type of player with differences in strength and imagination. The yardstick which usually distinguishes one from the other is how well each turns with the ball and who is most comfortable with his back to the opponent's goal.

The front man: The disadvantages of building attacks slowly are obvious. "Get behind the defence" is a sound piece of advice, but not an easy one to carry out. Quick, direct attacks are created and defensive pressure relieved by long clearances. But to whom? If the centre-forward and the wingers race off down the field their chances of receiving and controlling a long pass against a competent defence are negligible. Here is the value of a front man.

Many teams play one forward upfield who can be found easily with long passes from almost anywhere on the field which by-pass defenders and attackers alike. In this respect the front man is more like a centre-half, for he meets balls coming to him without necessarily having to control them. His object is to play the ball off to another attacker. It is often easier than the role traditionally expected of him if he is a striking centre-forward. And, of course, both roles are still within his scope. His value is now accentuated.

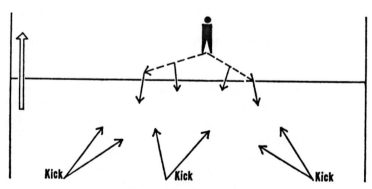

Fig. 9. The front man.

Making a long pass for a tall player to head is not so difficult. It need not be pin-point accurate. Ten yards either side will allow him time to move and meet it. But aimlessly flighted balls offer no problem to a defender.

A big man in this role is easier to find in trouble. A small man is less simple to hit accurately. Naturally he will not win so many balls in the air. Passes must be driven at him and he will need more control and great positional ability.

There is nothing new about this idea. Joe Mercer is always telling me that he was hitting Dixie Dean in 1932. Wynn Davies, Martin Chivers, Andy Lochhead, Hugh McIlmoyle and Frank Lord are all outstanding in this role. This sort of player works well alongside a colleague who can anticipate what he is going to do and help him by finding a good position between the front man and the defence. When John Charles was playing for Juventus the Italians could hit the ball up to him though he was surrounded by six or seven defenders. He always seemed able to get the ball to Sivori—and off they went from there. Lochhead and Chivers make many chances for other players in their attacks. John Ritchie is used much more as a front man for Sheffield Wednesday than he was at Stoke.

A good example of the smaller player as the front man is Johnny Byrne. His control and ability to lay the ball off is superb and this brought Geoff Hurst many openings in important West Ham matches.

The front man, obviously, is not limited to the centre of the field although this will give him more room. At Manchester City, Mike Summerbee, who has fine control under pressure, is sometimes used as a front man in almost any part of the field. But the other players must know where to find him in an emergency.

In less skilled football the job can be done effectively by an ordinary player if the opposition fall into the common trap of not marking a player who moves towards his own defence.

The coach's first question to himself will be: "What qualities have my players got?" A player's constant self-enquiry should be: "How am I playing?" It is not always easy for either to reach a realistic conclusion. Some players look good in practice and poor in matches and *vice versa*. Some are valuable for their size, weight, experience or personality. Every team needs within its framework a captain or somebody who takes charge at the back by character and voice. These are qualities which do not lend themselves to technical analysis. Trends, weaknesses and strengths can be revealed to the players and to observers more accurately through counts—a simple method of recording one player's actions during a match, on paper.

For example, assume the coach wants to know for sure which of the two wing-halves is the more reliable with his passing or is more constructive. Perhaps he feels one of them ought to be an inside-forward, or one of them should be pulled back to cover some other weakness. The passes each player makes are marked by someone watching the game. He writes down 8 if the ball goes to the inside-right, 9 if it goes to the centre-forward, 1 if it is back to the goalkeeper, 0 if it goes to the opposition.

This kind of cataloguing can be applied to each team player in all the physical aspects of the game . . . the goalkeeper's kicks and throws; can he kick to both sides of the field? Most goalkeepers are able to use only one side of the field for clearances because they can kick with one foot only. How successful are the full-backs' tackles? How accurate is their kicking? Can all the defenders kick a long ball? What develops from a winger's dribble? Or does it just look impressive? Can the centre-half head and where does the ball go? Which direction does the inside-forward favour with his passes? Does he always turn the same way?

The primary importance of counts is in making the player aware of his own characteristics. It is surprising—and players find this difficult to believe—how many footballers give the ball more to the opposition than to their own players.

When I first tried the idea with Manchester City players, with each reserve making counts on the player who was keeping him out of the first team, the League players thought it was designed to collect evidence which would lead to them losing their places. This was by no means the object. But the counts served as an inspiration before the first mark was made.

In one game against Sunderland we charted a comparison between Colin Bell and Jim Baxter, both playing somewhat similar roles in an even game. Baxter made forty passes and six of them went to our players. Bell made thirty-eight passes and only two went astray. At this stage Bell's confidence was low and evidence that he was more reliable than Jim Baxter could hardly be anything but flattering, although Baxter took most of the honours in the match reports.

In counts we took on Glynn Pardoe, analysing the direction in which he made his passes, we found that of his twenty-five passes twenty were sideways or backwards. He was as surprised as anyone and was able to halt a trend which could be dangerous for a full-back or a wing-half.

Ralph Brand, a striker of international quality and just as sharp and incisive as when scoring goals galore for Glasgow Rangers, was charted to be giving the ball away a frightening number of times. Rangers dominated most of their games and if they lost possession they would soon regain it. Ralph was valuable to them because he could score goals. But the Manchester City side he was playing in did not dominate in the same way. It was much more disastrous for them to lose possession.

In one Second Division match, Tony Book, playing at right-back, touched the ball sixty-three times and gave it away only three times. This is a model of consistency and accuracy to anyone.

Counts can be used for all kinds of match analyses. With hard facts at his finger-tips the coach will be aware of trends and actions before they happen, and during practice he can develop, correct or stifle them.

CHAPTER SEVENTEEN

System at Restarts

Restarts are as inevitable as the final whistle itself. Since they were originally included in the laws of the game to give one side an advantage over the other, it is a mistake to throw away that benefit by carelessness or lack of thought.

Restarts give the players with ability, imagination and method, scope to demonstrate all three. Acting, deception and pretence should be encouraged when the object is to deceive the opposition. It is the histrionics aimed at deceiving the referee which cause all the trouble.

Speed of thought and action are one of the most incisive weapons against any defence, never more so than at restarts. This means a quick kick or throw will often pay dividends.

But plans, counter-plans, decoy movements off the ball, and movements of geometrical beauty with the ball are so much wasted energy without the awareness and alertness of the whole team. Everyone must know what is planned and required, even if only two individuals are involved. If system at restarts does nothing else, it emphasises the theoretical principles of soccer and that it is a team game.

Kick-offs: a team which finds itself having too many kick-offs will need more than system at the restart to put things right. But it is worth looking into. Never does a team have more opponents between themselves and the goal than at a kick-off, making runs and elaborate plans more difficult. This should not stifle ideas, but it should temper them to be of the kind which depend on simplicity to exploit the weaknesses of the opposition's line-up—gaps, and squareness, as well as sleepiness.

There was nothing more simple than the move with which Spurs opened many of their home European Cup matches—

playing the ball back to a wing-half who put an up-and-under deep into the opposition's penalty area. With a capacity crowd willing goals and destruction all round, forwards converging on static defenders, and Bobby Smith bearing down on the spot where the ball would land like a two-legged tank run riot, it is hardly surprising that the opposition should feel that there was an advantage after all in having the first kick-off.

The idea of playing the ball back to the defender, apart from giving him space, will usually draw a number of the opposition away from their half. A long ball will by-pass them and make the most of the space and time the forwards have been offered.

Although generalisation is difficult, it is bad play to lose possession in less than four or five passes after a kick-off. If the opposition is an unknown quantity this is the quickest way of finding out something about them. Bearing in mind how early mistakes can unsettle a player, there is much to be said for immediate, direct aggression. A run and a long pass are not too difficult to conceive and execute, but almost without exception attackers are forced into harmless areas of the field by nature of the numbers stacked against them.

Do not expect too much from a kick-off without, at the same time, neglecting the advantage it offers. Do not overplan and do not forget the value of simplicity. Once ground has been gained, then the team can concentrate on pulling players and opening up the defence.

Line-up: offensively it will depend on what has been planned and what the opposition is doing. For the first kick it is not always necessary to have three inside-forwards bunched together on the centre spot. Nor is it economic to have the same three players grouped defensively. When the opposition have the kick-off, bring the wingers in from the touchline to discourage any straight run by the wing-half and to harry back passes. This leaves the opposition wingers with a certain amount of space, for the full-backs cannot both mark closely in this situation. If a team has to concede space, it is always better to do so in less dangerous areas and in front of a defender rather than behind him.

From the goalkeeper: the moment the goalkeeper has the ball, he becomes an attacker, not merely a defender with the biggest kick. His throw should give him greater accuracy and speed but less distance. Possession must be guaranteed from short throws and kicks, and they are dangerous unless the full-back or half-back is adept at receiving the ball. A short throw or kick—unless it is down by the goal-line, which is a slightly safer area, means the defender receiving the ball has to turn with the ball, a skill which most of them find difficult.

A team's plans from a restart involving the goalkeeper will depend on what he can do with the ball, not what he ought to be able to do. The vital principle is to create space into which he can kick the ball and into which one of his team will be able to move and meet the ball, sometimes to control and turn, sometimes to play it off to someone else.

The goalkeeper will kick either to the wings or down the middle. A player waiting to receive at the point where the ball lands is easy meat for the opposition. If the kick is designed for the winger he must first go too far into the opponent's half, where the full-back is obliged to stay with him. If the inside-forward has come well into midfield at the same time, the goalkeeper will have a large space into which to aim the ball . . . the space is his target, not a particular player. The winger then doubles back towards his own goal. If the full-back is unwilling to follow the winger, he can come deeper to pick up the ball. But he still needs the help of other members of his team to give him space.

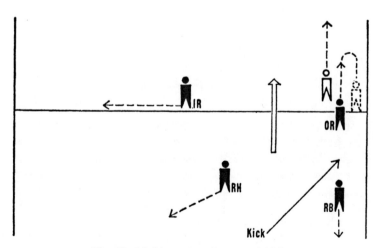

Fig. 10. Making space for a goal kick.

103

Space in the centre of the field is created in the same manner, by the centre-forward moving too far into the other half and the inside-forwards going 15 to 20 yards wider than usual.

Goalkeepers with particularly long kicks—and kicking out of their hands, using every inch of the area or with the help of the wind, they ought to be able at some time to reach an attacking distance—can spark off dangerous moves with an unusual tactic first exploited by Real Madrid, which is becoming increasingly popular with many leading teams. It entails kicking a very high ball down the middle at the opposing centre-half. One forward challenges and hustles him. The others, grouped around the area, converge on the defender and pick up the ball which he has been forced to head negatively instead of to a man. If an idea like this works in top-grade football, it will certainly work in lower grades of the game.

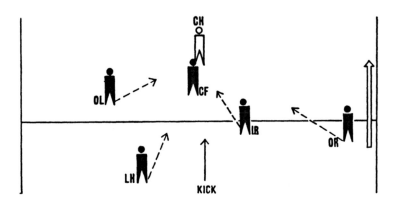

Fig. 11. Playing off an opponent.

It is taken for granted that most of the top-class goalkeepers can kick, and they only become noticeable when they kick badly. Many like Bonetti, Macedo and West, in the months when his thigh was troubling him, prefer to throw as often as possible. An ability to throw will never reduce the necessity of the goalkeeper practising his kicking and knowing exactly what he can or cannot do.

Throw-ins: space, once again, is the essence of a successful throw-in—and success means possession. It is bad play to lose possession at a throw-in and emphasis of this should discourage the throw-and-hope technique, common enough at all levels.

A quick throw will often gain an advantage and offensively a greater risk can be taken if there is a chance of more than just possession. In the defensive half of the field a quick throw can bring the goalkeeper into the game, but no risks should be taken. Apart from the danger of losing the ball in an area near goal, remember that the side taking the throw is temporarily outnumbered on the field.

One of two players, sometimes even both, is usually unmarked at a throw-in—the thrower or the full-back. The same man, the winger, will frequently have the impossible task of marking both players. The thrower is not in a position to make space for himself. Players standing well away from him, sometimes exaggerated distances, produce time, space and the opportunity for movement for themselves and the thrower.

On the other hand, watch a well-drilled team. If the players crowd in on the thrower it is a sure sign that the ball is going over their heads into the back space they have created to someone like the centre-forward or the winger.

Tricks from throw-ins are about as numerous as tricks at a Magic Circle meeting, although perhaps not quite so elaborate. Over-elaboration is less necessary, in fact, than simple disguise and unselfish movement. A quick interchange by the inside-forward and winger will leave space for someone; a player showing he wants the ball thrown to the right of him by touching that part of his shirt or shorts, then goes left and doubles back, will temporarily lose his defender and make space for himself; a man, like the other wing-half or inside-forward, coming fast from the other side of the field without fuss, can put himself in a position to receive the ball.

A long throw can produce immediate scoring chances. Frequently, however, it is over-employed or used as a type of weak corner with everyone crowding into the goalmouth. If it is brought into the game sensibly, aimed usually at the head of a forward positioned near the goal-line, he will be able to relay it into the goalmouth or win a corner from it. Once again space is a necessity. Swindon Town scored twelve goals in one season using Bobby Woodruff's throw-in this way. It can also be used in a similar way to the long goal kick—with attackers grouping

105

round a defender trying to head the ball away under pressure and picking up a half clearance.

The opposition's awareness of a long thrower's ability can leave him free to make a surprise run. When he throws, he is usually marked. If another player picks the ball up, the long thrower moves towards him as if to take the ball from him to throw it himself, and then overlaps him and sprints down the touchline, he can often be left clear to receive the throw himself.

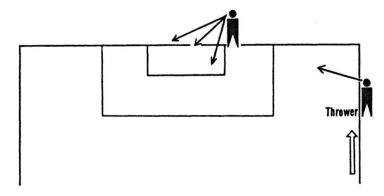

Fig. 12. The long throw.

Defensively, some professional teams, on the Continent particularly, prefer to contain the play within a small area and are prepared to concede possession rather than be caught out by more incisive moves. I prefer close marking with the thrower and a spare man goal-side of the throw. At a lower level close marking is certainly more profitable as it increases the chances of turning poor control into good effect.

Free kicks: as soon as the whistle blows to stop play, both sides momentarily relax. A quick free kick can exploit this temporary pause, but one player thinking quickly needs the support of others to gain an advantage. England's first goal in the World Cup Final showed just how important this is. Moore took a quick free kick "and found Hurst unmarked in the middle" some of the papers said. This explanation does both players an injustice. Moore certainly took a quick free kick; equally quickly Hurst saw what he wanted to do and ran a considerable

106

distance to meet the ball, accurately floated into the ideal spot for him to head in, unchallenged.

A free kick nearer the goal will usually be confronted by a wall. It is pointless for me to describe different ways of trying to beat the wall. There are far too many, and like everything else they depend on what the opposition is doing.

The principles, however, are these. A wall can be beaten direct from the kick only if it is badly positioned or the kicker can bend or dip a ball—and none of these conditions is common.

Since the wall cannot be moved, the ball must be moved to change the angle of approach whereby the wall will not impede a direct shot. Simple logic, but not always understood on the field. It means a side pass must be more than just a touch to put the players in the wall out of the game.

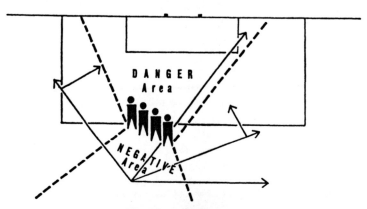

Fig. 13. Beating the wall.

Attackers always have the advantage, very rarely used sensibly, of running in on static defenders or at least defenders who are moving slower than they are. This is how the chip to the far post and the ideal situation of getting behind the wall will produce chances and goals. And in all these movements deception and disguise—false running, false calling, general hustle and bustle—will hide the most obvious plans.

Defensively: The number of players in the wall, made up of the wing-halves and inside forwards, will vary between two and five, but usually it is four. An extra man is sometimes included to project the wall outside the line of the posts if an opponent can bend a ball. It is the goalkeeper's responsibility, although an outfield player, usually a winger, must help him position it correctly. Defenders must, as always, keep an eye on attackers without losing sight of the ball. It is better to bring more players back into the area to close the gaps which invite attacking runs rather than to rely on anything so doubtful as offside. Never split the wall.

Corners: goals from corners are hard-earned and if they come at all they have the habit of coming when least expected. The first necessity is that it should be taken by someone who can kick correctly.

The man to avoid with the kick is the goalkeeper. If he picks the ball out he can eliminate five or six of the attackers from the game with a quick throw. It must go short of him, or beyond him, unless of course he is muffing everything in the air, then the nearer the goal the better. Forwards need to be able to run and meet the ball. They can afford to take a chance and anticipate the kick. Defenders are forced to keep an eye on attackers and the ball to see what both are doing.

The withdrawal of the forwards for the run will leave space in the area. The kick should go into that space. Usually corner kicks are not long enough. "Aim for the penalty spot." This is sound advice but frequently misinterpreted. If this is the target, the ball should go over the spot, to be headed, not land on it.

Leeds, Liverpool and Sunderland are three sides who call on their centre-halves at corners with the ball hit well beyond the goalkeeper to be headed back into the goal mouth.

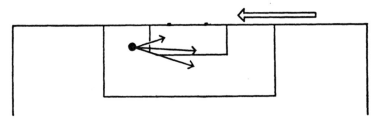

Fig. 14. The popular position for a big attacker at a corner.

Before the World Cup in Switzerland, the German international Fritz Walter spent eight weeks perfecting the accuracy of a rising corner kick which was met by a forward racing in as the ball passed over the penalty spot.

The most fashionable corner at the moment first appeared in its best form in the last World Cup. Bene ran from the back of the area across the face of the goal to meet a driven ball with his head. He gave the impression of running too far and too fast, for he was always well past the edge of the goal area and not far off the goal-line when he met the ball. This was not within the goal-keeper's reach and a slight deflection gave him a very good chance of a goal or a rebound.

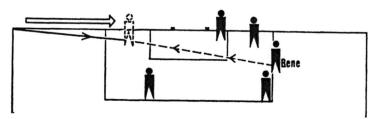

Fig. 15. The Bene corner.

One of the few players who scored goals without a run was Bobby Smith. He was not always a good positional player, but he seemed to put the ball in the net regularly with a standing jump, and the goalkeeper on top of him.

On bad pitches, with a heavy ball, and for younger players, the short corner has many points in its favour. Playing it back to a defender with more time and space will often overcome some of the disadvantages.

Defending against a corner entails denying the opposition the opportunities we have mentioned before. Two full-backs inside the posts who remain on the line to give the goalkeeper cover and more freedom of movement; close man for man marking, positioned in such a way that each man can see the ball and his opponent; the nearest two players to oppose attackers trying a short corner—one is not enough and will be beaten easily. Attackers making runs must be shadowed. The Bene-type run can sometimes be spotted by an alert full-back on the near post; the most dangerous attacker must be marked by someone capable of beating him. But beware other defenders are not drawn towards him, neglecting their own responsibilities.

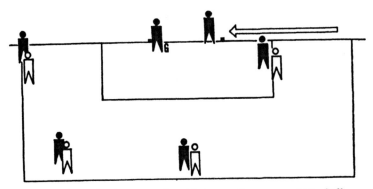

Fig. 16. Defenders must be able to see the man and the ball.

John Charles, in his early days at Leeds as a centre-forward and a centre-half, took up exactly the same position at a corner whether he were defending or attacking—on the far corner of the goal area. This was the best place from which to pick his run, heading in or out. And it is also a good example of the rule of giving the stronger players priority. Not everyone can have the best position.

CHAPTER EIGHTEEN

Making Things Happen
(with the ball)

The difference between a team playing well when they have the ball and a team merely playing reveals itself in the number of players who want the ball and the number who can receive the ball at any given moment. It should be the same number, somewhere between one and four.

Hard work makes easy play when work means unselfish running. At the beginning I brought in the fundamental principles of the team game—sensible running, going to help a player with the ball, outnumbering the opposition, running off the ball. This goes hand in hand with confidence, calling and enthusiasm to get into the game. The object is to make the game as simple as possible for the team, and as difficult as possible for the opposition. Keep them moving and struggling to weigh things up.

Enthusiasm and fitness will take a player only so far. During the 1950 World Cup Billy Wright was marking Didi. The Brazilian ran 30 yards into a space. Billy Wright went with him. The ball did not come. Didi ran 40 yards. Billy Wright went with him. The ball did not come. Then 30 yards and the same thing happened. The fourth time Didi ran 35 yards into a space Billy Wright went only half-way with him. The ball went straight to Didi!

No doubt this sort of thing was happening all over the field. Whoever gave the ball to Didi appreciated the situation. Good running needs awareness all round—and praise. If it goes unnoticed too long it will cease completely, particularly when the game is going wrong. By 1966 the Brazilian team were playing as if skill alone won matches and had reduced their running. In the adversity of the World Cup most of them stopped running and left Pele and the younger players with some impossible tasks.

Improvisation will always win more openings, for nobody is quite sure what will happen. That often includes the players improvising unless practice and training has brought complete understanding. Here is a selection of simple set plays which might increase the chances of an opening.

1. The wall pass should already have come quite naturally into the earlier small games. If it did not, players have not understood the basic idea of running.

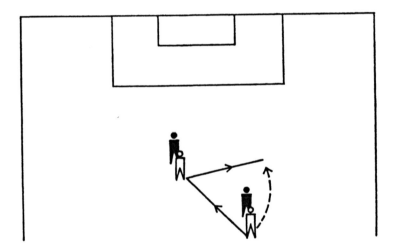

Fig. 17. The give-and-go of the wall pass.

2. Closely marked forwards can take defenders underneath high balls or to one side of passes, anything to make their judgement falter.

3. Check-outs—the simplest and most underrated way of making space by running one way, usually away from the ball and taking the defender, then checking suddenly and changing direction.

4. Cross-overs—the scissors movement of rugby which has two variations. A player crosses in front of the man with the ball and either takes the ball from him or runs straight through without the ball. The one who keeps possession is usually the one facing the goal.

5. Overlapping—usually on the wings. A full-back or wing-half feeds the winger who moves forward and away from the touchline, taking his full-back with him, while a player runs round the outside, down the wing to receive a pass. This is the present most popular way of beating a packed and retreating defence, although good defences are learning to block it. Chelsea and West Ham do it well, McCreadie and Peters particularly; Cohen and Armfield have played it for some time.

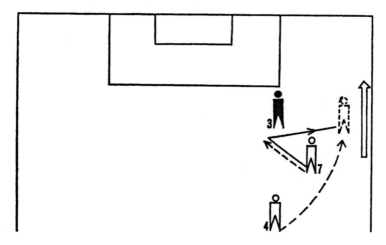

Fig. 18. Overlapping (by number 4).

Good football does not consist of playing 10-yard passes up and down the pitch and then having shots blocked off in the penalty area. Nor is it a matter of hitting long passes all the time.

Assuming they never reach perfection, teams will always play too much of one or the other. Results are not always an indication of whether a team is playing well, although victories seem to indicate that they are playing well enough. West Ham have for some seasons been playing some exceptional football. Ron Greenwood's problem was stopping them from giving away goals in defence. Errors like this are usually obvious and they are the first things to correct.

In general, play and passing are the most important single skills in the game. They are indications of how well a team is playing.

Do they have possession a lot? Are they making movements of three, four, five and six passes? Are they making chances? When they lose possession are they regaining it quickly? If the answer to these questions is 'Yes', then some sort of basic football weakness is letting them down. If the answer is 'No', then bad passing will have something to do with it. Inaccuracy is not the whole answer. Here are one or two do's and don'ts which might help.

1. Try to look for the far man first, as Puskas was always saying. If a pass to him is not possible or accuracy cannot be guaranteed, find someone nearer.

2. Always look for a winner. But don't always try it. Don't be over-ambitious. Be realistic. Keep the ball moving quickly.

3. Don't be clever. Be either good or safe.

4. Don't be averse to safe or negative passes. Safe angles mean somebody else is helping and the ball cannot be cut out or the receiver dispossessed. A safe or negative pass gives the passer an opportunity to find a better position.

5. It takes a good player to go to a safe angle. Arthur Bellamy, the Burnley half-back, is exceptional at this. Every side needs players like this. They make the other players look good. The England side a few years ago consisted of players who looked good but weren't, and players who made the others look good and were good themselves. Some of the really big names belonged to the first category, the less heralded ones to the second group.

6. Some potentially winning passes will be intercepted because they are the hardest to make. If it is a deep ball only one person will be cut out of the game. A through ball is easier to control, but if it is cut out the opposition can attack immediately. A floated ball beyond the defence will take longer to return.

7. Short square passes are obvious. If they are cut out, two players are immediately out of the game. Long, square passes on the ground are dangerous. A long, accurate pass which switches play is excellent in theory, of course. A floated ball or a chip is safer, in practice.

8. Habitual big kickers will gain ground but lose possession. Stop them by conditioned games with no goals, the object being the total sequence of passes.

9. Habitual short passers are predictable and lose possession even more. Stop them by conditioned games—long passing, no crossing the half-way line.

10. Individualism is important, but in the right places, within the striking area. Individualism in mid-field is easier, but simple teamwork is better.

CHAPTER NINETEEN

The Sweeper

So far I have talked in general terms about system. Now I want to particularise on one of the most important but least understood aspects of team play, defensive system.

The pivot defence, the WM formation and traditional up and down running remain popular because they are common and part of players' upbringing. I do not believe this particular formation is either the best or the easiest to grasp. Players are left with too many doubts, above all the centre-half in defensive situations and the full-backs and wing-halves in defence and in attack.

The dual centre-half system of 4-2-4 is fashionable and gives better cover and more freedom. But it offers space to an inside-forward in front of the last line of defence.

Sir Alf. Ramsey is one of many who has stressed the need for more all-round players. Young players usually have all-round qualities until specialisation produces uneven development. At any age or level full-backs and wing-halves often have an unexploited talent for constructive play when the ball is in front of them. And having emphasised throughout the previous chapters that forwards should be encouraged and bullied to work harder in defensive roles, it is a natural corollary that the work load should be evened by giving some defenders more responsibility and freedom to join in attacks.

This would be impossible in the pivot defence without sacrificing cover. Some other systems achieve this but rely too much on the ability of two, three or even all ten individuals. The team organisation which, I feel, suits most levels of play and provides cover and freedom is the sweeper system.

The basis of the defence using one man as a sweeper is man-for-man marking. The centre-half marks the centre-forward or striker. The two wing-halves mark the inside-forwards. The full-backs mark the wingers, closely. If the centre-forward moves out of the middle the centre-half goes with him. Similarly, the other defenders follow their men wherever they go unless this involves a radical positional change for a long period, in which case they change with another member of the team who would be more comfortable there.

The sweeper's job, operating behind them, is to provide cover for all the players, particularly the back three. He is a substitute defender, standing by in an emergency to cover mistakes, break-throughs and through passes.

The pattern of the majority of his running will be across the field. When an opponent makes a forward break alone or gives a through pass the sweeper should normally be in a position to cut out the pass or close on the player making the run.

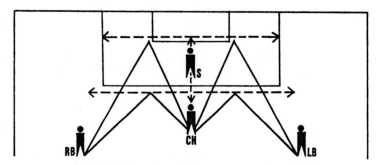

Fig. 19. The sweeper's pattern of movement.

In the face of an attack outside the penalty area the sweeper places himself between defenders to make a rough triangle of cover.

He must beware of running too deeply into the no-man's-land between the goalkeeper and the last line of defence. When the attack has reached the danger area, close to the goal, he should position himself in such a way as to be part of the back line, the limit of retreat, and cover the middle, by tucking in behind the centre-half. The temptation is to make the triangle of cover in the usual way, but this allows opponents space to run off the ball very close to goal.

117

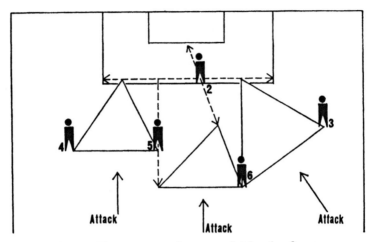

Fig. 20. The sweeper makes a rough triangle of cover.

When a defender is beaten the sweeper immediately goes to the opponent who is free. This is not the job of one of the other defenders unless they are within tackling distance. Too many men are left unmarked, perhaps only for a fraction of a second, if other defenders try to engage the attacker, for this involves switching positions and roles. They will have their own problems keeping close to the men they are marking.

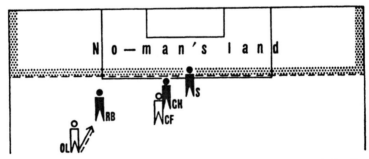

Fig. 21. The sweeper, the last line of defence and no-man's land.

The advantages are that the quality of cover for the centre-half is incomparable with the pivot system. (The full-back on the far side can still come away from his winger to give a little more cover.) There are no free men in defence. It compensates for any error or weakness at the back. It offers double cover to most of the defenders. It is a stimulating position to play.

Certainly, this reduces the number of forwards to four. But the full-backs, and to a lesser extent the half-backs, have been freed from much of their territorial restriction. Full-backs particularly can commit themselves more to attack—overlapping, helping the winger and the middlemen, at throw-ins and corners, never to the neglect or exclusion of their responsibility for the winger or the flank, but without the worry of being the only cover for the centre-half and middle.

Fig. 22. The sweeper takes the spare man.

This, in turn, calls for different qualities from those which would make a successful, traditional full-back. If defenders are to be asked to join in attacks effectively they probably need a higher grade of skill. They should not be uncomfortable at the front, nor must they be without experience and practice of attacking situations, like shooting and centring. Facchetti, the Inter-Milan full-back, is probably the prime example of the success of freeing an aggressive defender to join in attacks by means of this kind of system.

With a sweeper to cover them, all five of the marking defenders can break out into attack. If the left-back joins an
attack the sweeper temporarily takes his place. If two or three

Fig. 23. The sweeper substitutes for a defender who has joined the
attack.

defenders break away he takes up the most glaringly open position. Well-trained opponents will chase defenders in these situations. The lazy ones take their time moving upfield. Here, the
sweeper either marks a lazy player or pushes up far enough to
leave him offside. This is not so much a tactical move as an in-
surance against idle opponents gaining an undeserved advantage.

What sort of a player makes a sweeper? He needs coolness
and an ability to read the game. He should be a good kicker and
passer of the ball, for in a match he will find himself in possession a great deal and able to get himself out of trouble only with

120

a long pass. The position is a test of character. It is possible to fill the role adequately without doing a great deal of work. On the other hand, a conscientious player will cover a wide amount of ground and be in the game much more than the centre-half or full-back. For attackers fail to make allowances for him and play into his hands.

At Maine Road, when we began to operate this system, we had a centre-forward and a wing-half as full-backs, an inside-forward and a wing-half as the wing-halves; the centre-half was playing in his natural position; the sweeper who was originally a full-back was capable enough to play anywhere defensively.

The forwards were made up of a genuine midfield player of ability, two wingers with wider responsibilities and covering considerably more ground than conventional players in these positions. One was upfield and wide, the other was deep and used all the flank. Despite the predominance in defence of players trained in attacking positions the problem was not conceding goals but scoring them. We created plenty of chances and brought in a variety of centre-forwards in an effort to turn them into goals.

Junior players at Maine Road adapted themselves surprisingly easily to the idea of the sweeper and enjoyed the extra running and freedom. The youngest players averaged more than four goals a game in the first season. Stan Bowles, then seventeen and a professional, was first picked to play the role and he performed it well. But as the club's most accomplished midfield player at that level he was of more value farther upfield. Tom Booth, seventeen, an amateur, training only twice a week with few of the team he played with on a Saturday, then became the sweeper in the "A" team and the Youth side with great success. He was normally a wing-half without much speed but completely composed.

I cite these examples to make it clear that although the sweeper is a specialist role, its application is not beyond younger players with a reasonable appreciation of the game. And young defenders revel in the chance to be more constructive.

In the World Cup Schultz, the West German captain, Rattin and Troche, the Uruguayan captain, played the role of sweeper. The dual centre-half system is more popular in League football. The rare example of the sweeper, and it could hardly be bettered, is Bobby Moore. Chelsea also use it well with Marvin Hinton as the sweeper, although he gave way to the young full-back Jim Thomson on occasions.

CHAPTER TWENTY

The Breakdown Period

This is the instant or age between the ball changing possession and each individual changing gear. In good teams it is a fraction of a second, in bad teams an age. Awareness, alone, of this period by all the players will improve a team's play. Many footballers stop, relax, stand, look, decide, and then act when the ball changes hands. If these separate actions can be reduced the benefit is sometimes quite spectacular. Chelsea, Leeds, Liverpool and Manchester United work hard at this problem.

It is obviously much more vital when a team loses possession, although the Uruguayans strove to exploit this period when they gained possession. One or two players were detailed to attack at great speed from the rear at the instant their team won the ball. The remainder backed up as quickly as possible to leave idle opponents out of the game.

The breakdown period is largely one of the coach's duties. It is questionable whether it should get more than a passing reference in amateur and junior football. The lower the grade the more the ball changes hands. Players who reacted immediately to every breakdown would be exhausted after a few minutes' play.

In more general terms it becomes a question of concentration. Even at the highest levels this could be improved. If Bobby Charlton has a fault it is inconsistent concentration. Jimmy Greaves, on the other hand, told me he can make himself concentrate in a game to the extent that even when the opposition are about to gain possession near him he expects them to make mistakes and is prepared to snap up the chance—when the goalkeeper drops the ball, when the centre-half misheads or a defender miskicks. Maintaining concentration of such intensity for ninety minutes is most demanding.

Man-for-man marking in small games emphasises the breakdown period. The ball will change hands every three or four moves, involving a change of role and mental outlook.

CHAPTER TWENTY-ONE

Making Things Happen
(without the ball)

A team losing possession is in trouble whether the players realise it or not. They have lost the initiative and they must regain it as soon as possible.

Losing possession in attack: Young players are not terribly concerned about losing the ball in the opposition's penalty area. Tommy Docherty's only criticism of Peter Osgood in his early days with Chelsea was that he grinned apologetically if he did something wrong near goal.

Often, the nearer a team is to goal the more players will be put out of the game by losing possession. A cross intercepted in the penalty area will eliminate between two and six players. If there are only four left and one makes a desperate tackle and is beaten, the team's plight sinks from unhappy to unhealthy. The formula must be: can you get the ball back immediately? Usually the answer is no.

Mark tight in the area of the ball.

Cover at the back.

Forwards should get behind the ball or behind the half-way line.

One or two players will be unable to get back. One or two forwards, however, should be detailed to get back every time. This will encourage them to play with a certain amount of depth behind the other forwards. In an alert unselfish team, these roles will often be interchanged.

The speed with which players put themselves between the ball and the goal is important to sides playing a system which frees players to attack. Sometimes as many as seven or eight players are in an attacking area within 30 yards of the goal . . .

although eight is too many, I feel. If seven cannot get through it is unlikely that eight will.

Whatever happens, they must not put themselves out of the game by trying desperate tackles. An occasional surprise run by a strong determined forward might dispossess a defender. Mike Summerbee achieves some good results in this way. A chaser might harry a defence into mistakes. Jimmy Greenhoff, of Leeds, perhaps not a natural centre-forward, has been used in a lone nuisance defensive role at the front. This extra running will reduce the effectiveness of a forward. It would be unwise, for instance, to expect it of someone like Greaves.

If players can get behind the ball when it is still in the attacking half, then they can become more aggressive by trying to frighten the opponent into making a bad pass. They can even try a tackle.

Tackling alone is like jumping out of a front-line trench and taking on the enemy single-handed. It can be done, I suppose, by the Dave Mackays and Billy Bremners of football, the villains and the V.C.s of the game. It is much easier and less foolhardy to get the ball back collectively . . . other players hovering nearby as the tackle is made.

Closing the game up: The object is to cut down the area of vision and space of the opposition. A defence on a football field, as on a battlefield, needs depth and width. Cover and basic positional play should always give depth. As for width, a football defence, unlike a military defence, can only be attacked at one point at a time. By closing into a much smaller area than normal—the men farthest from the ball pushing over the most—attackers are forced to try and beat someone. Their play is restricted as if the size of the pitch had suddenly been reduced.

A full-back in the pivot system has always had to sacrifice some width for the sake of cover. I am advocating that this should be done by all players, not necessarily with cover in mind, but to close the game up.

The distance a player pushes over is limited to whether he can regain touch with his opponent if the ball is suddenly switched.

If play down the defensive right flank is switched, the right-back or wing-half could be free to receive the ball. The outside-left or left-back should still be able to regain contact, even though a tackle would be impossible. The rest of the team then push over together in support.

Pushing over must be performed quickly. There is always the danger that a good opponent will spot the tactic and turn it to his team's advantage by hitting a quick long pass in the transition period while the players without possession are moving into their closed-up positions.

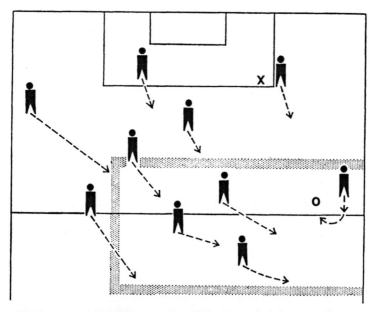

Fig. 24. Attack intercepted at X; before the opposition have worked the ball to O the side without possession have closed up into roughly the shaded limits.

Jockeying: not from four or five yards; move closer, a yard or two from the man with the ball. Make him do something. Some defenders run half-turned because they put themselves so close to their opponent. Some full-backs have developed the technique of turning inwards when the ball is pushed outside them. This is a question of which foot they prefer to push off with and which way they are already turned.

Shepherding: it is possible to invite or force attackers into less dangerous areas or areas where a tackle is easier. By standing off a winger, for instance, when the play is on his side a full-back can encourage an inside-forward in a more dangerous position to pass to the winger. Or the full-back can make the winger come inside or outside according to how he jockeys him.

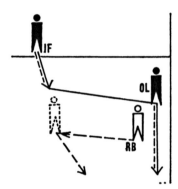

Fig. 25. The right back encourages the inside forward to pass to the winger by moving inside.

The danger area: Anywhere in the last third of the field, around the penalty area, the if's and but's must stop. Every action must be part of a collective movement. Cover must be there, tackles must be made. Here, there are no safe situations while the opposition has the ball. It is less dangerous on the wings, but not if the wingers are allowed to centre the ball.

Controlling a good player: When an opponent is continually beating his man in the danger area something must be sacrificed, usually far cover, to stop him. The confidence and timing of a player who has been beaten once or twice deteriorates sharply. By close support from behind he must be given confidence that he will get the ball in the tackle. He jockeys until the man in support sends him into the tackle with a quick word of command. If the defender is beaten the second man will normally be able to make an immediate tackle. Often the first defender will begin to win the ball because of his improved confidence. The danger of this sort of activity is that too many defenders will be pulled out of position.

Losing possession in defence: whether this is through over-confidence or lack of skill the net result is equally serious,

128

primarily because of the area, secondly because when one member of the defending team has won possession the other defenders relax because they are thinking in terms of attack.

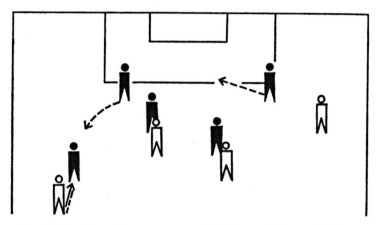

Fig. 26. As the extra man prepares to help control a good player, the far defender gives cover in the middle.

The goalkeeper should never be caught unawares, but for the other players nothing less than immediate reactions will save the situation. The most common reaction at losing the ball in defence is to stop with an "Oh no, not that" expression. Once again this brings in the question of the breakdown period.

This problem emphasises how important it is for players to be dedicated to the idea of clearing the danger zone quickly, coolly, firmly. Put safety first, with safe passes and safe angles, which usually means long balls to the wings or to the front man.

Printed in the United Kingdom by
Lightning Source UK Ltd., Milton Keynes
138314UK00002B/138/P